MARRIAGE LAWS, RITES, RECORDS & CUSTOMS

WAS YOUR ANCESTOR REALLY MARRIED ?

Colin R Chapman

FIRST EDITION

LOCHIN PUBLISHING

The cover illustration by Nick Ind is based on "The Sacrament of Matrimony", a woodcut in *The book* Intytulyd *The art of good lyvynge & good deyng* translated from the French by Samoht Notgnywel (Thomas Lewynton) and published on 30 May 1503. The original *Le liure intitule l'art de bien viure et de bien mourer* was published by Anthonie Verard in Paris in 1493 with the same woodcuts. Until the Reformation in the British Isles, marriage was considered the seventh Sacrament, as explained in Chapter 4. Other illustrations in this Cameo are also by Nick Ind.

Warning! Do not use this book seeking to gain a legal marriage, legitimacy, inheritance or divorce today. Obtain up-to-date guidance from a professional lawyer. Adopt only those wedding customs which are not injurious to health in the present century.

Published by
LOCHIN PUBLISHING
6 Holywell Road, Dursley, GL11 5RS, England

First Edition 1996 (1 873686 02 1)
Reprinted with minor alterations 1997
Copyright of the Lochin Publishing Society 1996, 1997

British Library Cataloguing in Publication Data
Chapman, Colin, 1939-
Marriage Laws, Rites, Records & Customs
(Chapmans Records Cameos Series)
1. Marriage 2. Marriage law 3. Marriage customs and rites
I. Title
306.8'1
ISBN 1 873686 02 1

Contents

Preface

As a teenage organist I was able to observe scores of weddings of a variety of Christian denominations from many an organ loft, wondering at the tears being shed - invariably more profuse than at funerals for which I also played accompanying music. I later discovered (see Chapter 8) that tears are a good sign. With my chums I enjoyed riotous engagement parties and pre-nuptial celebrations, but a Quaker pal had introduced me to the more sober wedding ceremonies of his faith. And a Jewish friend allowed me an insight to the customs associated with his marriage. I was Best Man to an old school friend who entered wedlock in true English traditional style at the Anglican parish church of his bride followed by a hotel reception, and also at the marriage of a Methodist friend in the chapel where he and his bride were regular worshippers, after which the reception was held at the home of other friends.

Whilst living in Guyana I attended arranged weddings within the Hindu and Moslem faiths, and I played a variety of instruments at celebrations of Holy Matrimony attended by the highest Roman Catholic to the lowest Evangelical congregations. In the East End of London I was the equivalent of Best Man at a Sikh wedding, the associated festivities of which included chartered coach trips to Cardiff and Bedford and continued for well over a week (but being younger, I had more stamina then). I was guest of honour at the Buddhist wedding of a Burmese friend to his Japanese wife followed by tea drinking, though I am still unsure if I enjoyed the raw fish also consumed afterwards. More recently in Indonesia I have attended some vivacious Javanese weddings with mystic sounds from gongs, unklung and gamelang.

It was, therefore, with some first-hand experience of different marriage rites and wedding ceremonies that in 1990 I began writing this Cameo. In collecting material I quickly realised I needed an understanding of how matrimonial lawyers had worked in the past. I spent months struggling with Wilkins' *Concilia* (see Chapter 2) published in 1737, mostly in Latin; this diverted my attentions to the sin, sex and violence of the Church Courts in which those lawyers practised. My Cameo on Ecclesiastical Courts, Officials and Records thus overtook the present work, fundamentally completed in 1992. But I slowly sank among my voluminous notes on matrimonial legislation, the hundreds of English and Welsh, Scottish and Irish Parliamentary Acts dealing with marriage, and the thousands of pages of commission reports and of Bills that never reached the Statute Books. Several Cameos later, after Pauline Litton and I had shared some lectures in America on using marriage and other records, she came to my rescue.

Editing my original text proved impossible and, giving me even further information, Pauline conduced me - beyond encouragement - into re-writing the entire text, but then mercifully provided invaluable assistance in commenting on and verifying many details. This Cameo is complemented by her own booklet *Basic Facts on Using Marriage Records* (see Bibliography), outlining the practicalities of research among these records.

Throughout this Cameo, when referring to monetary values, I have quoted pre-decimal units in use before 1971. Those readers to whom these mean little should read my Cameo on old weights, money and other measures: *How Heavy, How Much and How Long?* The various words associated with marriage, used in the opening paragraph of this Preface and throughout the Cameo, may require some amplification. Matrimony, Holy or otherwise, tends to be the more formal term employed, particularly in legislation, whilst marriage and wedlock (less commonly heard today) usually describe a couple's position and life-style. Wedding includes the formal ceremony, the nuptial blessing or mass, and the subsequent jollifications, the reception and associated customs.

Sadly not all marriages are happy or permanent unions today. Many commentaries are written in attempts to explain why the divorce rate in the British Isles is now 160,000 times higher than the low rates in the 17th, 18th and first half of the 19th Centuries. The structure of the family, the rights of men and women, legitimacy and adoption are all facets of the fascinating debate intimately linked to marriage, but are minefields for the unwary. I decided not to enter that debate. Notwithstanding, in this Cameo there is some information on past divorce and matrimonial disputes in the ecclesiastical and civil courts, and I have touched on legitimacy and adoption. Importantly for potential researchers, I have indicated where records of all these may be found.

This Cameo is based on my British research. To include here details on laws, rites, records and customs of religions other than formerly practised within the British Isles or using references from too far beyond these shores would have resulted in a massive tome too academic to assimilate, too heavy to handle and too costly to purchase. For fun I have included some pranks traditionally performed at weddings and I have listed some anniversaries and gem-stones and colours associated with such occasions; I believe that some trivia is not out of place, even amidst the solemnity of marriage.

Thus in the following pages you will find the reasons for many present matrimonial laws within the British Isles, the origins of many marriage rites, the whereabouts of marriage records and the backgrounds to many customs enacted during courtship and marriage over the centuries.

COLIN R CHAPMAN.

1. An Overview of Marriage in the British Isles

Alongside the hundreds of delightful customs associated with courtship and marriage there are equally hundreds of turgid matrimonial laws and edicts emanating from Church and State. Many wedding customs are simple adaptations, or in some cases embellishments, of pagan rites and superstitions, whereas most marriage laws are rather convoluted. In addition some matrimonial terminology is obscure and can be quite daunting. Even the terms marriage, matrimony, wedlock, nuptials and wedding can be equivocal, unless you have read the Preface! Nevertheless, an awareness of marriage law, modified from time to time, as unfolded in Chapter 2, is helpful in our understanding of why a couple and their families reacted out of character - at least that is how it often appears in the records they have left for us to reconstruct their lives. The chapters which follow include outlines of important laws associated with marriage in the British Isles, some features affecting the validity of marriage and divorce, and a selection of those rites and customs of courtship and marriage whose origins have a degree of credibility.

Some may ask why we, or our ancestors, should care about being married or undergoing a valid marriage anyway. For many couples, apart from the moral issue, it was probably of little legal consequence, particularly if they had no possessions, real or personal, to pass on to their children. In the past, however, all parishioners knew each other and they were not going to be denied the fun of a possible wedding. Furthermore, since 1236 [1.1], a child of an unmarried couple is illegitimate and, under the Poor Laws, bastards (who cannot inherit) were a potential drain on parish funds. It was, therefore, in everyone's interest to encourage courting couples to enter wedlock. Only from 1927 [1.2] in England and Wales did subsequent marriage legitimate a bastard (and even then, only under particular circumstances - see Chapter 2). Remember also that every child born to a married woman has always been her husband's legitimate child, even if the couple has been apart for years. It was, therefore, for practical reasons, rather than respectability, that a couple aspired to undergo a valid marriage; and furthermore, through a record of some sort, wanted to be able to prove that they had. Hence an entry in a marriage register was useful, better if witnessed, and more so with written confirmation. For those of us today who use evidence of marriage to research social or family history, such records are vital - so vital in the USA, at least, that marriage, birth and death documents are officially termed "Vital Records".

A couple planning to get married in the past often drew up, with guidance from their families, a contract or settlement regarding the rest of their shared lives. If the bride, in particular, was bringing a dowry in the form of land to the partnership, this was specified in the documentation, normally with meticulous references to former owners of that land and surrounding properties. Dowries and marriage settlements (and dower for a widow, though abolished in 1925), though intended to be of material benefit to a couple, were regarded by neither Church nor State as

3

essential for a valid marriage. Nevertheless, many marriage settlement papers and contracts, whilst generally personal documents, have survived throughout the British Isles. These deeds and documents, of exceptional value in historical research, are described in Chapter 6.

In our overtly secular present century it is easy to forget the strong influence of the Church on our ancestors. Education, social security, probate and certain aspects of law and order were all handled by ecclesiastical authorities. Even proving one's very existence or demise was easier if a baptism or marriage or burial had been recorded in a church register - which was feasible from 1538 when parish registers were introduced. Some marriages were noted even before 1538 in monastic registers and chronicles, but such notes are so few and far between they need not concern us here. Parish records over 100 years old should now [1.3] be kept at County or similar Record Offices in proper storage conditions of humidity and temperature. Registers have been filmed and scanned and microforms made available in libraries and archives around the world. Entries from many registers have been transcribed by individuals and local and national societies and indexed alphabetically under names and places. A great deal of this material has been published [1.4] on paper and in microform and, more recently, on CD-ROM and the Internet.

From 1597, copies of parochial events, including marriages (and baptisms and burials) were required by the Church authorities. Such copies or transcripts should have been made in each parish every week and sent annually, via the archdeacon, to his bishop for deposit in the diocesan registry. Not all parishes complied (and some were outside this requirement anyway) and so in many cases these extremely useful Bishops' Transcripts (BTs) are not available. Nonetheless, they should always be sought, even if the parish registers are extant, as some entries appear in the BTs which were not recorded in the original registers. In some parts of the country, the copies for the early 17th Century survive and the registers do not. All BTs and most parish registers today are kept at county record offices, unless there is a separate diocesan registry. In Ireland some priests made similar copies, Parochial Returns, in the 19th Century but retained them in their parishes - see Chapter 7.

Apart from an earlier, brief period of civil registration from 1645 to 1660 during the Interregnum period (see Chapter 2), civil registration of marriages (and births and deaths) by the temporal authorities commenced in England and Wales in 1837. In Scotland and Ireland civil registration of marriages began in 1855 and 1845 (see Chapter 7), on the Isle of Man in 1884 and in the Channel Islands at various times from 1840. The exact dates and present whereabouts of these records are clearly stated below or in *Tracing Your British Ancestors* [1.5].

Another civil statute in 1837 - the Wills Act [1.6] - hinged on the validity of a marriage. By this Act, still in force today, every will made by a man or woman is revoked by his or her marriage. Exceptions apply only when certain powers of appointment are identified. The 1925 Law of Property Act [1.7] permitted another exception for a will made expressly in contemplation of matrimony. Hence from 1837 to 1857 the Ecclesiastical Probate Courts wrestled with the validity of marriages before some wills could be considered for probate or Letters of Administration granted. From 1858 [1.8], the civil probate courts had to solve such problems.

Long before and well after the Reformation, English monarchs and Parliament constantly referred matrimonial disputes to the Church Courts for arbitration and judgement. However, disputes over property that a wife brought to the marriage and any debts incurred (her debts - and credits - were her husband's liability) were dealt with at Common Law in civil courts, as were some cases of injured feelings, although Church Courts dealt with defamation. On occasions Chancery Courts also became involved when Equity Law was encroached upon - for example, married women retaining their own property in trust, disputes over alimony and marriages of orphans and lunatics who were wards of Chancery. Nonetheless, William I (in 1072) and Edward III (in 1344) both stated that bigamy, bastardy and similar matters required exclusive ecclesiastical solutions; specific Matrimonial Courts to deal with such problems were opened only in 1858 [1.9]. Before then, if the civil authorities did become involved, it was normally to confirm a decision already made by a Pope (prior to 1534) or by an Archbishop, Bishop or one of their representatives (after 1534). Accordingly, church records are a useful starting point in locating evidence of marriage.

The qualifications for a legal marriage, based on a mixture of ancient Roman, Germanic and Canon Law, and the impediments to a valid marriage, including age, being in an existing relationship or Holy Orders, and the approved place and time for a wedding, are explained in Chapter 3. Whilst many denominations of the Christian Church and Jews practised their own rites and ceremonies from the 16th Century in Britain, normally only marriages performed in a parish church, apart from those of Jews and Quakers, came to be recognized by the English and Welsh authorities. The Jewish and Nonconformist positions are described in Chapter 5; those in Scotland and Ireland are explained in Chapter 7.

Divorce, the converse of marriage, was legally impossible in England and Wales after the Reformation until 1857 except through a private Act of Parliament, as outlined in Chapter 9; whilst not so expensive as some commentators claim, it was nevertheless a complicated procedure. And so ecclesiastical court lawyers used every possible ruse to demonstrate that the initial marriage was somehow void (had never really existed in law) so permitting the couple to legally go their separate ways. This, naturally, made the children illegitimate and their inheritance invalid, another disincentive for divorce in the past, but apparently tolerable for the very few couples who chose this path before the middle of the 19th Century.

Notwithstanding, the temporal authorities did dabble in matrimonial matters before 1857 when they saw an opportunity for raising revenue. A Lord of a Manor, under the feudal manorial system, required his tenants to seek his permission before they married or organised marriages of their children. When permission was granted the tenant had to pay a merchet duty, termed a fine, in the form of cash payment or rendering a service or providing a proportion of the fruits of toil. This not only acknowledged the Lord's authority and responsibility to look after his newly-wedded tenants (he provided certain facilities and protection), but conveniently added to the manorial inventory. The Lord rarely attended tenants' weddings but occasionally he paid for the festivities. Amongst manor court rolls, the records of court deliberations, it is possible to find evidence of the manorial marriage duty being paid, by whom, how much, in what form and under what circumstances. The antithesis of the merchet was leyrwrite, a tax for unchastity (sometimes termed incontinency or adultery). The Lord of a Manor felt justified in imposing this as it represented a breakdown in the framework of the manorial community. Origins of, and customs associated with, the merchet and handling unchastity on a manor are described in Chapter 8.

With comparable enterprise, monarchs and governments grasped every opportunity to tax their subjects and the electorate, often to fight a war, usually against the French. Hence, from time to time, particularly from the late 17th Century, either the marriage ceremony itself, or the written entry of the marriage in a register, or the paper or vellum or parchment whereon the event was recorded, were chosen as suitable items on which to levy a duty; a financial penalty was imposed if the duty was not collected. Such pecuniary secular interference, in areas for which the Church was totally responsible, was neither welcome nor successful - in fact for those of you who delight in utilizing marriage records today in your research, it was a disaster as many, quite valid, marriages passed unrecorded, merely as a means to avoid paying the tax. Even some Welsh curates in St Asaph and Bangor Dioceses took a tenth of the goods of both parties on marriage; but this dissuaded so many couples from wedlock that the tithe was declared illegal in 1549.

In the first millennium, soon after Christianity began to influence life in the British Isles, the Church encouraged two possible routes to marriage: after the calling, reading or publishing of Banns (see Chapter 4), or following the grant of a Special Licence by the Archbishop of Canterbury or of a Common Licence by an archbishop or bishop or a representative of one of them. Such encouragement can be seen in decrees from the Pope and his legates in Britain until the Reformation; indeed, existing Canon Law is based extensively on these decrees. Publishing marriage banns and granting licences continued uninterrupted in most parts of the British Isles after the Reformation, as the Protestant Anglican Church promoted these same routes to matrimony. Only in areas of Scotland, where neither residual Catholicism nor new Anglicanism had strong influence (see Chapter 7), did the acceptance of banns or licences (in particular) tend to lapse.

Unfortunately, throughout most of the British Isles, the clergy were lax in recording the calling of banns or the granting of licences, particularly the former; it fell to the temporal intervention of Oliver Cromwell in 1645, and a century later of Lord Hardwicke, to remind the people of these practices. Hardwicke made it a civil and legal requirement for a valid marriage in England and Wales to have, and to record, either the calling of banns or granting of a licence. He also introduced some novel concepts to matrimonial law, as described in Chapter 2. We should not forget, however, that publishing banns and recording this fact is no guarantee that a marriage later took place. Nevertheless, records such as banns books or the documentation associated with marriage by licence - the allegation (application), the entry in the bishop's book, the bond (agreement) and the licence itself, can prove useful when looking for the subsequent marriage entry. These documents are likely to be in county record offices or equivalent archives today.

An additional source of information on a wedding, after the 17th Century, is a report in a newspaper or periodical and, from the early 19th Century, a trade magazine. When a notable couple was involved between 1750 and 1850, a synopsis of the report is likely to have been published (and indexed) in the *Gentleman's Magazine*. From 1763 to 1862 the *Annual Register* [1.10] also published noteworthy marriages in increasing profusion. Larger public reference libraries and some archives have copies of their local newspapers, the *Gentleman's Magazine* and the *Annual Register*. The British Library Newspaper Collection [1.11] has extensive sets of local and national papers and periodicals. Scottish and Irish holdings are identified in Chapter 7.

Marriage On & Over the Seas

Although this Cameo concentrates on wedlock in the British Isles, it is thought useful to include here some brief notes on marriages of British subjects on and over the seas. Separate Statutes [1.12], not elaborated upon in this Cameo, covered such nuptials. Records of marriages conducted on HM ships, and at British consulates and embassies, were sent to the Registrar General in London or to the Foreign Office. These records, some indexed, are now in the General Register Office (GRO) [1.13] or the Public Record Office (PRO) [1.14]. The Bishop of London assumed responsibility for some Anglican churches abroad, not under the jurisdiction of a particular bishop. Many of those records are in the Guildhall Library, London [1.15], some are in Lambeth Palace Library [1.16], and others are in the British Library, Oriental and India Office Collection [1.17]. Nonconformists of every denomination embarked on many missions overseas, recording marriages and other events in registers; copies or originals of some of these records are held in the British Isles by the missionary or denominational historical societies. Many marriages of British subjects abroad are recorded only in local registers around the world. The Guildhall Library has published a booklet on this topic, *The British Overseas* - see Bibliography.

Some marriage registers and records in the PRO relating to British subjects on or over the seas:

Army Officers and their families	WO 42		Naval Officers returns	ADM 13
Admiralty registers	ADM 7		Passengers at sea	BT 158
Correspondence and papers	RG 48		Royal Artillery	WO 69
Gloucester Regiment	WO 67		Royal Garrison Regiment	WO 19
Greenwich Hospital School	ADM 73		Royal Marines, Chatham	ADM 183
Irish Tontines	NDO 3		Royal Marines, Plymouth	ADM 184
Isle of Sheppey	ADM 6		Royal Marines, stations	ADM 6
Militia	WO 68		Royal Marines, Woolwich	ADM 81
Miscellaneous	RG 32, 33, 34, 36		Ships' Logs	BT 165
(the Misc. from 1627-1960 are indexed in RG 43)			Soldiers' documents	WO 97

Some Consulate records, including marriages, with Public Record Office reference numbers:

Adana	FO 609	Foochow	FO 665	Paris	FO 630
Amoy	FO 663	Galati	FO 517	Peking	FO 564
Barcelona	FO 637	Hankow	FO 666	Ponta Delgada	FO 559
Batum	FO 397	Ichang	FO 667	Port-au-Prince	FO 866
Bremen	FO 585	Iran (various)	FO 923	Riga	FO 516
Bremerhaven	FO 586	Isfahan	FO 799	Rostov-on-Don	FO 398
Brussels	FO 744	Kalinigrad	FO 509	Santo Domingo	FO 683
Budapest	FO 114	Kunming	FO 668	Sao Paulo	FO 863
Buenos Aires	FO 446	Lausanne	FO 910	Shanghai	FO 672
Bushire	FO 560	Leipzig	FO 299	Shimonoseki	FO 797
Cantagena	FO 920	Leningrad	FO 378	St Vincent *	FO 767
Chengtu	FO 664	Lisbon	FO 173	Stockholm	FO 748
China (various)	FO 681	Loanda	FO 375	Tabriz	FO 451
Chinkiang	FO 387	Montreux	FO 911	Tallinn	FO 514
Cologne	FO 155	Moscow	FO 518	Tientsin	FO 674
Curacao	FO 907	Nagasaki	FO 796	Tripoli	FO 161
Damascus	FO 684	Nantes	FO 384	Tsingtao	FO 675
Dresden	FO 292	Ningpo	FO 670	USA (various)	FO 700
Dusseldorf	FO 604	Oslo	FO 529	Vladivostok	FO 510
Edirne	FO 783	Papeete	FO 687	* Cape Verde	

The PRO holds some marriage records from former African and Asian Protectorates (RG 33 and RG 36), Denmark (FO 211), Istanbul (FO 441), Japan (FO 345), Odessa (FO 359), Reunion (FO 322), Saxony (FO 218), Seville (FO 332), Switzerland (FO 194) and Tristan da Cunha (PRO 30/ 65). Some marriages appear in the West Indies Slave Compensation Papers (NDO 4) and in some Garrison records (WO 156).

*   *   *

In 1732 "an ancient author" assured that "all women, in the eye of the law, are either married or to be married..."; there was obviously no thought of any woman choosing by design to remain single and develop her own career. "...and their desires are subject to their husbands, as a man shall forsake father and mother to stick to his wife. The principal causes of matrimony are these two; increase of children, and the avoiding of fornication and uncleanness; and whosoever marries for beauty, riches or other motives, rather than those before mentioned, are said to be guilty of a crime, tho' not expressly disallow'd by our law" [1.16].

Readers of this Cameo may already be identifying the category into which they fit! The following chapters offer further information, but not legal advice, on matrimonial matters and where the associated records of the past, and in some cases copies and indexes, may be found.

2. Legal Milestones Affecting Marriage

Background

Matrimonial Law in the British Isles evolved over the centuries from an assortment of sources. There were the decrees of the Witenagemot which was the Council of Wise Men, secular and spiritual leaders, who had met at Pentecost and Easter from Anglo-Saxon times. There were Papal Bulls, Letters and Rescripts, and the Constitutions of Otho and Othobon, the Pope's legates, and Constitutions of various Archbishops of Canterbury and York. There were letters and canons of bishops, and decisions resulting from ecclesiastical synods held at national, provincial and diocesan levels. And there were royal grants and charters relating to the Church and extracts from monkish historians. All these, and many other legal statements, were conveniently assembled and published by David Wilkins in 1737 [2.1]. From such a medley, it was no wonder that marriage law was complicated and even today lawyers argue on what was, and is, intended.

Simply, as explained in Chapter 3, it emerged that a legal marriage anywhere in the British Isles required only mutual consent and agreement ("self-marriage") between a man and woman to become and remain faithful as husband and wife for the remainder of their lives. For centuries, a ceremony, priest or other celebrant, witnesses and festivities were unnecessary [2.2]; nonetheless, spiritual leaders were constantly urging that all unions should be sanctified by the Church.

As mentioned in Chapter 1, questions on the legality or validity of a marriage were normally passed swiftly from the temporal to the ecclesiastical courts. The laws were certainly complex and the temporal courts were far too involved anyway with earthly matters such as land ownership and tenancy and finance. This was expressly the situation prior to the Reformation and, as often quoted, King Henry VIII's marital difficulties were a contributing factor in England and Wales to the break from Rome. Henry anticipated the Pope, as Head of the Church on Earth, would grant him a "divorce" (actually an annulment of the marriage - see Chapter 9) from Katherine of Aragon to enable him to marry Anne Boleyn. But the Pope had already bent the rules in permitting Henry to marry Katherine (at the time of their betrothal they were both under age and, furthermore, she was his deceased brother's widow - both impediments to marriage as explained in Chapter 3) and the Pope had no intentions of being compromised again. In addition, Mary Boleyn, Anne's sister, was Henry's mistress and the affinity impediment (see Chapter 3) should have barred Henry from marrying Anne anyway. A pictorial representation of Henry's solution to his immediate problem is on page 64 of this Cameo.

There were, of course, very many other reasons, beyond the scope of this Cameo, for disaffection with the Roman Catholic Church, and Henry merely mirrored fractious thoughts; but in 1534 he declared himself Head of the Church in England thus founding the Protestant, Anglican, Church of England. Scotland was then a separate kingdom with its own monarch, and it was another three years before Henry attempted to convince Ireland of his logic; at this time, therefore, his jurisdiction affected only England and Wales. Scots and Irish positions on matrimony are discussed in Chapter 7. This chapter applies mainly to England and Wales, although most Statutes mention only England: from 1535 laws in England applied also to Wales following the Law in Wales Act [2.3].

A new era had dawned and hereafter the Crown and later Parliament felt they had a right, if not a duty, to comment on or even interfere in ecclesiastical judgements. Even the King's Bench in 1682 declared that "divines know better how to expound the law of marriage than the common lawyers" [2.4]. Henry's second marriage most certainly caused bewilderment in the minds of those who thought they understood canon matrimonial law: the rules as stated in the Bible appeared no longer to apply in England and Wales and clarification was needed. Thus in 1533 the first of many media releases from Reformation times to today relating to marriage was published as a Statute (see below). Since then there have been hundreds of further laws affecting marriage, many not even carrying the word marriage in their titles. In a "user-friendly" book of this size, it is sensible to dwell on those laws which are outstanding; this will assist you who are interested in using marriage and its records to study the story of a community, or to research the history of a family and the antics of its individual members. Accordingly, the legal milestones only are outlined here. Those of you who would study in depth other laws affecting marriage should refer to the many other Statutes quoted in Appendix I.

Laws of the 16ᵗʰ & 17ᵗʰ Centuries

Many policy decisions on marriage, from various Popes in Rome and from archbishops and lesser officials of the Christian Church, were published over the centuries - see Wilkins [2.5] for details. The Bible was used as the basis for many decrees and edicts and pronouncements, including prohibited matrimonial relationships identified in the book of Leviticus [2.6]. The Council of Trent (1545-63), convened within the turbulent and divided Roman Catholic Church by Pope Paul III at Trent (now in Italy), debated matrimony, among many other matters of dogma. However, England had already severed ties with Rome and, as mentioned above, the initial temporal Statute regarding marriage was issued by Henry VIII in 1533 [2.7]. This spelt out for the first time in English civil law, kindred whom one should not marry (tabulated in Appendix II of this Cameo). The Act also mentioned that Marriage Licences could be granted by the Archbishop of Canterbury. Unfortunately there was some ambiguity in the wording of the Statute regarding in-laws; so another Statute [2.8] was passed in 1536, extending prohibited kindred to include all relatives of any woman whom a man had carnally known. These two Acts really only re-stated the Levitical prohibitions, using slightly different wording, but replaced living wife's sister with wife's sister. Still there was confusion and so later in 1536 [2.9] another Statute was introduced which quoted kindred prohibited by God's Laws declared in the Bible or otherwise in the earlier 1536 Act.

For four years no one could work out who was legally able to marry whom; thus in 1540 yet another statute [2.10] was enacted, in effect saying that all marriages were valid unless prohibited by God's laws. However, in 1553 [2.11] Queen Mary, a devout Roman Catholic, repealed the first two of Henry's Acts, and in 1554 [2.12] the second pair was repealed. By the Supremacy Act of 1558 [2.13] Protestant Queen Elizabeth I restored the second pair only of Henry's Acts, implying that solely the Levitical degrees of impediment now applied. But as the second 1536 Act referred to the first 1536 Act, and the emphasis on a wife's sister was not the same in both Acts, it was, even then, not absolutely clear what was intended. To quell all further confusion, Archbishop Parker (of Nosey Parker fame) in 1563 cited sixty prohibited relatives (see Appendix II) in an Admonition, based on his (Purity of Reason) interpretation of the Levitical degrees; in 1603 this was embodied in Canon 99. Although prohibiting a broader range of kindred than Henry VIII had identified, there was now no dilemma over descriptions used for various relations. Those 60 prohibited relatives for a valid marriage remained for over 300 years until modified by the temporal government in 1907.

During the English Civil War (from 1642), Parliamentarian passions were so inflamed that their opposition to the "Establishment" included both Monarchy and Church, the latter established and headed by the English Monarch for just over a century. Ardent Puritans, abhorring the ornamentation in some parish churches, vandalized that and some records, including a few marriage registers. The Welsh churches were particularly badly abused, Cromwell's men stabling their horses in St Asaph's Cathedral and Merthyr Tydfil church, using fonts as pig troughs and lighting huge bonfires with documents from the St Asaph diocesan registry and Llandaff Cathedral library [2.14]. In 1643 a meeting of Parliamentarian extremists in the Jerusalem Chamber of Westminster Abbey, and so tagged the *Westminster Assembly*, declared birth, marriage and death to be secular matters and that baptism, marriage and burial as then practised by the Church should cease. (In the same year, in Scotland, the *Solemn League and Covenant* defined a similar reference to ecclesiastical reform - see Chapter 7). The Assembly approved instructions for The Better Observance of the Lord's Day; these were adopted by Parliament and introduced on 8 April 1644 "for the peace and safety of England, Wales, Scotland and Ireland". Rules for the Ordination of Ministers were issued on 4 October of that year. From 4 January 1645 *The Directory of Public Worship* replaced *The Book of Common Prayer*. There was to be provided:

"...at the charge of every parish or chapelry in this realm of England and dominion of Wales, a fair Register Book of velum, to be kept by the minister, and other officers of the church, and...shall be written and set down by the minister therein...the names of all persons married there and the time of their marriage;...and that the said book shall be shewed by such as keep the same, to all persons reasonably desiring to search for the...marriage...of any person therein registered, and to take a copy, or procure a certificate thereof".

The *Directory* also gave instructions on the solemnization of matrimony, impediments, ages of parties, banns (though the word "purpose" was used), and guidance on the minister's homily and the words to be spoken by the groom and his bride. The requirement to keep carefully a register "for the perusal of all whom it may concern" was included. 1645, therefore, marks the first statement in a civil directive of the need to publish banns before a valid marriage. Although Canon Law had urged this for at least 400 years, until now a valid marriage had needed only a verbal contract, assuming there were no legal impediments.

To reinforce the impediments from 24 June 1650 a Parliamentary Act [2.15] also named forbidden kindred "for the suppressing of the abominable and crying sins of adultery and fornication, wherewith this land is much defiled and Almighty God highly displeased". Couples who married within the prohibitions were guilty of felony, for which the penalty was death; their marriages were void and children of such marriages, however solemnized, were illegitimate. For a similar Act in Scotland in 1649, see Chapter 7.

An Act on pretended marriage was passed in 1651 [2.16]; this enabled Lords Commissioners to annul and declare such a union void, if they were convinced a bride had been forced into marriage against her will. But it would seem that neither this, nor the 1650 Act, nor the rulings in the Directory were sufficiently clear. So in 1653 [2.17] Parliament imposed (effective from 29 September) *An Act touching Marriages and the Registering thereof; and also touching Births and Burials*. This stated that names and abodes of both parties, and of their parents, guardians or overseers, had to be given in writing to a locally appointed Parish Register (registrar) 21 days before the intended marriage; this allowed for the required three successive publications (of banns) in the parish church or market place, which for validity had to be between 11am and 2pm.

The 1653 Act further required the subsequent marriage to be conducted by a Justice of the Peace in the presence of two witnesses. This introduced a purely civil ceremony and eliminated any spiritual involvement from the legal matrimonial knot. The ages of marital consent were prescribed as 16 for males and 14 for females (although parental consent was needed for those under 21); instruction was given on where and how the marriage ceremony should be conducted (see Chapter 4), and what records should be kept "in the Commonwealth of England". The Act required the true and just recording of publications (banns) and marriages, and births and burials, "of all sorts of people" in a vellum or parchment book by a Register (registrar) elected (by contributors to the poor rate) for a 3-year term from 22 September 1653, and approved by the

Justices. A shilling marriage registration fee was payable (births and deaths [sic - not burials] were only fourpence each to register) as was a similar fee for publishing banns and for a copy certificate; the poor were exempt from fees. All earlier registers were to be given to the new registrars for safekeeping as records.

At the Restoration of the Monarchy in 1660 the pre-Civil War matrimonial legislation was re-instated, although the Acts of 1644 to 1653, including the secular requirement to publish banns, were not specifically repealed. The former parish register books were brought out and dusted off (if they had not been destroyed, the case in some parts of the country). Some incumbents had persisted in conducting their services and sacraments contrary to the dictates of Parliamentarians, and had continued using the original parish register books; those marriage entries flow on as if nothing had happened. A series of entries from 1653 to 1660 in identical and relatively tidy handwriting may indicate events being entered retrospectively after 1660 from memory or rough notes; thus those details may be less reliable. In a few instances of marriages of persons from different parishes, there is more detail in one parish register, so do look at the registers of both parishes. Some couples did not believe their marriage was "proper" if a magistrate had performed the ceremony; they went to the nearest parish where a clergyman was continuing to celebrate Holy Matrimony in defiance of the Puritan ordinance. In many parishes, however, registers contain few marriage entries after 1642 and none after 1653 until 1660.

When marriage records formally appeared again in Statutes it was only coincidentally, but usefully for researchers today, as a method of ensuring compliance with some new tax laws. In 1694 Parliament passed a Stamp Duty Act [2.18], attempting to help finance wars against France. A tax was imposed on vellum, parchment and paper for four years from 28 June 1694; this included "for every skinn or peice of vellum or parchment or sheete or peice of paper upon which any licence for or certificate of marriage or any letters of mart shall be ingrossed or written, the sume of five shillings". A marriage licence was referred to only as a document to be stamped as an income source and, understandably in a Stamp Act, no guidance was given on the requirement or validity of types of licence. Commissioners were appointed and other officials were to keep accounts and pass collected money to the Exchequer every Wednesday. Financial penalties were payable for every conceivable deviation from the minutiae of the statute; forging the stamp or mark, or selling counterfeit stamped parchment, was a felony punishable by death.

The 1694 Stamp Act failed to raise the anticipated revenue, and William III needed further funds to fight the French "with vigour". Hence, later in 1694, Parliament approved a more extensive duty [2.19], effective from 1 May 1695, intending to raise cash during each of the following five years, fortuitously for us also generating certificates [2.20] and requiring register entries.

This tax was imposed on each registration of marriage (and also birth and burial, and on bachelors and widowers). Paupers were exempt. The Act included a clause that persons could be married in Peculiars only with a licence or after the publication of banns; this was to improve the collection of duty on licences and certificates under the 1694 Stamp Act, then still in force. (A Peculiar was similar to a parish but was outside the jurisdiction of the usual ecclesiastical authorities. This clause was added because of the concern that more and more couples were marrying in Peculiars, at "lawless churches", without the publicity of banns or the granting of a licence. Although this did not produce void marriages, since the 1660 reinstatement of pre-1645 requirements, it went against canon law which tended to be observed in most other parishes. There were other clergy in London and elsewhere, who also took advantage of the 1660 legal changes - see below). The duties, graded according to social class, and fines payable are given in Appendix III. This Act is constantly misrepresented in modern textbooks: baptisms were not identified as events to be taxed, although to better levy and collect the duty, the clergy were to keep a register of every person married, buried, christened or born "...to which book or register the collectors for the respective parishes and places and all other persons concerned, shall have free access to view the same at all reasonable times, without any fee or reward".

The 1694 Marriage Duty Act (as it is usually called, although other features were also taxed) was to be implemented by Commissioners named in the Subsidy Act [2.21] passed earlier in the same session. They were to meet in their respective counties on or before 30 April 1695 and address precepts to two inhabitants of each parish, whom they considered fit persons to act as assessors, to appear before them within ten days. They were then to fix a day on which these assessors were to bring in certificates with full names, estates, degrees, titles and qualifications of all persons living in their respective parishes. The certificates were to show, in columns, the qualities and names of all persons chargeable under the Act and the sums they were liable to pay on marriages, births and burials and for being unmarried. The assessors were to return the names of two collectors, for whose honesty and ability the employing parishes were to be responsible.

The certificates were to be returned to the Commissioners before 13 May 1695 and a duplicate assessment delivered to the Receiver-General of the Revenue. The collectors were to deliver, annually, a certified copy of the assessment to two local Justices of the Peace who, after due examination, were to sign it as approved and to hand it to collectors whom they appointed for the ensuing year. These collectors were bound to deliver a true copy to the parish incumbent within six days, or pay a fine; the incumbent was similarly bound to read out the copy in the market place or in church on the following Sunday immediately after the morning service (identical to the Parliamentarian method of 50 years before to publish banns). Appeals against the assessment had to be made within ten days of the reading.

Many clergy simply annotated their existing registers rather than obtain new ones specifically to comply with the Act. Some entries are marked with 'P'; whether this indicates tax 'Paid' or 'Pauper' (tax not paid) is not evident straightaway. This Act had three immediate effects:

- a rise in the number of designated paupers (it is unclear if these really were paupers or a sympathetic clergyman exempting some parishioners from payment);

- a fall in the number of entries, and hence taxable events, in marriage registers (which may indicate a fall in events being recorded, not in valid marriages being conducted);

- a further rise in marriages taking place in Peculiars and extra-parochial and non-parochial churches and chapels; all such places fell outside the normal jurisdiction of the ecclesiastical authorities for a number of reasons. Some couples even left England and Wales for marriage to elude the jurisdiction of the Act.

To avoid charging or collecting the duty some parish clergy sub-contracted marriage solemnization to their unbeneficed colleagues. As before the 1694 Stamp Act, some extra-parochial churches and chapels believed they were exempt also from this Act and, by offering duty-free marriages, attracted many couples. Scotland, and to a lesser extent other places not subject to English and Welsh law but within reasonable reach, allured other couples. Several celebrants in London, such as the chaplain of the Fleet Prison and the clergy of St James' Duke's Place and Holy Trinity Minories, chose to believe, or may even have believed, that they had a wonderful market in banns-free and licence-free marriages. Other "marriage-mongers", "hedge priests" and "couple beggars" operated elsewhere up and down the country. The Fleet prison [2.22] was used especially for debtors but, having insufficient accommodation for all offenders, prisoners who could find surety lived in private houses or lodgings nearby. The duty-free appeal, as at airports today, even sheer devilment enticed couples from all strata of society to these areas.

Marriages conducted in all such places were often away from the bride's or groom's normal residence, useful to hide a physical deformity, but two further complications arose: firstly the ceremony did not gain the usual publicity of a local event, thus the marriage was said to be in secret or clandestine; secondly, the residential qualifications (see Chapter 3) of the bride and groom were not satisfied and so the marriage was irregular. An irregular marriage was later defined as one for which banns had not been published nor a licence granted. Colloquially (but strictly incorrectly) both a secret and an irregular marriage, whilst either could be valid, became termed clandestine.

Among those living within "the rules" of the Fleet (the area around the Old Bailey and Ludgate Circus) were clergy deprived by the Church Courts [2.23] of their livings for misconduct, though very few were in prison themselves; many, like the prison chaplain, were quite prepared for a fee to conduct clandestine (and some fraudulent) marriages. The Establishment responded swiftly and an Act in 1696 [2.24] claimed that "ministers, being in prison for debt or otherwise, do marry in the said prisons many persons resorting thither for the purposes aforesaid, and in other places for lucre and gain to themselves". Other clergy without benefices or permanent livings, who were being used by incumbents to perform marriages on their behalves to avoid the Marriage Duty

Act, were brought within the provisions of the 1696 Act. Incidentally, this Act also recognized that Nonconformists were not having their children baptised, and thereby not recording their births. Accordingly provision was made for these children to be registered. The 1696 Act also imposed restraints on marriages without licences or banns, and encouraged the better registering of marriages (and births and burials); a few parish registers reflect this.

In spite of its many problems, the 1694 Marriage Duty Act created some splendid records for researchers today. As mentioned above, every clergyman, under a financial penalty, was required to keep a register of all persons married (and buried, christened and born) in his parish, and of bachelors over the age of 25 and of widowers. It also required assessors to prepare certificates or lists. Just about everyone, apart from spinsters and widows, was taxed and listed, thereby generating the equivalent of a nation-wide 1695 census. Unfortunately no centrally-maintained lists were kept and for many counties they have been lost; even so some valuable lists have survived, as described in the Chapmans Records Cameo on Pre-1841 Censuses [2.25].

Laws of the 18th Century

Whilst not containing one word on marriage, the Parliamentary Acts [2.26] leading to the Union of Scotland and England eventually became effective on 1 May 1707; nevertheless, matrimonial matters having application in Scotland were henceforth debated in the Westminster Parliament. From this date, therefore, it is to that forum that we must turn for details on Scottish marriage law.

Many incumbents failed to collect the duties payable under the Stamp and the Marriage Duty Acts of 1694; hence further Acts of Parliament in 1705 [2.27] and 1711 [2.28], were introduced to encourage them to do so. The 1694 Marriage Duty Act was extended to 1 August 1706, well beyond 1700 - the originally planned date, so our chances of finding references to our ancestors in these records should be higher. The 1711 Act required the use of proper register books with ruled and numbered pages, but few parishes appear to have heeded this and the matrimonial trade around the Fleet continued. By 1723 the *Weekly Journal* [2.29] reported this business to be so prolific that even some taverns in that part of London had paid clergy on their staff. The King's Bench prison was almost as notorious: irregular and clandestine marriages were performed in their thousands here and elsewhere in London, as mentioned above.

The registers and records of places like the Fleet were purchased by the government in 1821 and deposited in the registry of the Bishop of London. Commissions were "appointed to inquire into the state, custody and authenticity of non-parochial registers or records of births or baptisms, deaths or burials and marriages lawfully solemnized". Their report (18 June 1838) led to the 1840 Non-Parochial Registers Act [2.30], following which the records were transferred to the Registrar General [2.31]. The report of a second commission on 31 December 1857 led to the 1858 Births & Deaths Registration Act [2.32], causing further records to be deposited - see below.

In 1753 Chancellor (Lord) Hardwicke introduced his famous Act [2.33] *"for the better preventing of clandestine marriages"* in England and Wales, making all marriages void unless following the requirements of the Act. It prescribed methods of publishing banns, granting licences, conditions for conducting a legal and valid marriage ceremony and maintaining registers. Hardwicke's Act, whilst formally breaching the canon law of marriage, was primarily intended to curb the vast numbers of irregular, though many valid, marriages conducted particularly around the Fleet in London without banns or licence. The Act did not apply to the Royal family, to Quakers or Jews, or to marriages performed in Scotland (or Ireland, not formally in the Union then) or beyond the seas. As this Act is perpetually misquoted in many genealogy books, most sections of it are summarized in the following paragraphs.

For a valid marriage from 25 March 1754 banns were to be published (using the words from the *Book of Common Prayer*) on three Sundays preceding the marriage, at morning service in the parish church or public chapel where banns had customarily been published, and where the couple resided. If the parties lived in different parishes, the banns were to be read in each parish or chapelry; if they lived in an extra-parochial place, banns were to be read in an adjoining parish or chapelry. The marriage could be solemnized in a parish only where the banns had been read. Certification of the banns being read was to be in writing in the parishes of publication or, if in an extra-parochial place, in the adjoining parish.

The couple planning to marry by banns had to give the parson at least seven days notice with, for each of them, Christian and surname, address and length of residence there. Parental consent was needed if either party, unless a widower or widow, was under 21; if the parents objected and the parson went ahead, he was to be punished by an Ecclesiastical Court, the banns publication void and the subsequent marriage null and void. A Common Licence to marry in a parish church or public chapel could be granted by an archbishop, bishop or a representative, only if at least one party had lived in the associated parish or chapelry for four weeks immediately before the granting of the licence. The right of the Archbishop of Canterbury to grant a Special Licence remained as set down in Henry VIII's Act of 1533 [2.34].

Anyone solemnizing matrimony otherwise or elsewhere than identified in the Act, and prosecuted within three years of the offence, could be found guilty of felony and transported to America for 14 years (the vicar of Great Houghton, Northamptonshire protested in his register "a punishment little inferior to ye gallows..."), and the marriage was null and void. However, after the marriage, proof of address under publication by banns and proof of four weeks' residency for a licence was not necessary, and any contrary evidence would not affect any suit regarding the validity of the marriage. In addition, the Church Courts were not able to compel a marriage "in the face of the church", even if there had been a contract of espousal or betrothal of present or future words (this was a significant change from previous tradition - see Chapter 3).

To ensure there were "no undue entries and abuses in registers", Hardwicke's Act required churchwardens to provide proper books of vellum or good and durable paper in which banns and marriages were to be registered. Every page was to be numbered at the top, beginning with page 1 on the second leaf. The numbered pages were to be ruled with (as near as possible) equidistant lines, with entries written on (or conveniently near to) the lines. Books were to belong to the parish or chapelry and to be carefully kept and preserved for public use.

All marriages were to take place in the presence of two or more credible witnesses besides the celebrant. A register entry was to be made immediately after the ceremony, stating whether by banns or licence (and if by licence and either party was under 21, that parental consent had been given), and stating the names of the parson, both parties and two witnesses. Anyone found forging a marriage entry was guilty of felony and was to be punished by death.

The entire Act was to be read in all parish churches and public chapels on one Sunday a month in September, October, November and December 1753 and on the Sundays preceding 25 March, 24 June, 29 September and 25 December for two years following 1 January 1754. As the original Act is quite long, this must have left little time for a sermon or perhaps resulted in a few burned Sunday lunches. The Act defined the temporary end-point in England and Wales of valid marriage by a simple mutual exchange of vows without witnesses; but its prescriptiveness caused couples with opportunity and resource to go to Scotland, Ireland, the Channel Islands and elsewhere, as some had done following the 1694 legislation, and others even earlier.

In the event Hardwicke's Act created almost as many problems as it solved and there were several attempts in subsequent years to have it repealed. Nothing had been put in place to ensure compliance with many of its requirements - well over "*57 Varieties*" of registers were published employing differing printers [2.35]; this provided anything but consistent information on couples and their marriages, and created some voidable marriages (see Chapter 3). The Act was attacked in the House of Commons as an unwarrantable invasion of the liberty of the subject; it was also held to violate feminine delicacy by prescribing public weddings: "The most shocking thing", Fanny Burney (1752-1840) asserted, "in the whole world". In 1765 the Act was repealed by the Commons but the repeal ignored by the Lords. In 1772 it was again successfully repealed in the Lower House, but on condition that an amendment be made in committee; after the required change was made, the House turned around and rejected the repeal. In 1781 another attempt failed in the Commons, and so Lord Hardwicke's Marriage Act remained substantially in force into the 19th Century - although some clauses concerning banns were modified.

A Bill laid before Parliament in 1758 to levy a tax on marriage (and other) entries made in parish registers to raise cash for the Foundling Hospital failed. In 1782, however, George Box's Stamp Duty Act [2.36] did reach the Statute books, whereby from 1 October 1783 every entry was subject to a 3d stamp duty. Paupers were exempt and were to be given a certificate stating this.

The clergyman, or whoever entered the event in the parish register, was empowered to collect the duty, receiving two shillings in the pound for his trouble, but having to pay £5 if the duty was not paid. The churchwardens had to provide books in which to enter the stamps indicating that duty had been paid. In practice the Collectors of Duty frequently granted printed licences to incumbents to make entries in their books without stamps, on condition that the duty was actually collected and entered into the Register Book.

By this time religious toleration was in the ascendancy and some Nonconformists had their own registers, although only marriages actually celebrated in an Anglican Church were valid, apart from those of practising Quakers and Jews. But Box's Act applied only to parish registers of the Established Anglican Church. Thus in 1785, by a further Act of Parliament [2.37], the provision of this duty was extended to Nonconformists at their insistence; they believed this would add formality to, and aid official recognition of, all their registers so putting them on the same footing as parish registers. In the event, Box's and the 1785 Acts proved extremely unpopular for Anglicans and Nonconformists alike, even though not applying to paupers. Many parties either did not pay the duty or failed to go through the ceremony which occasioned an entry in the register. Likewise the clergy were placed in awkward positions by having to extract money from their impoverished flocks; this caused some clerics to pay the duty out of their own pockets whilst others performed the ceremonies but did not record them in their registers. Irregular and clandestine marriages thus poured back until this unfortunate Act was repealed [2.38] in 1794.

The 1782 and 1785 Acts, applying to both the Established Church and Nonconformists, created some separate records - such as the licence granting exemption from the duty. In general, however, the Acts caused a fall in registered marriages, until repealed in 1794. If it is any consolation to readers of this Cameo, the absence of a marriage (or baptism or burial) recorded in a register between 1783 and 1794, as is the case with the situation from 1694 to 1705, may not mean that the event did not take place but simply that it was unrecorded. A marriage, therefore, may have been irregular, but not necessarily void; but unless its merits were debated before a competent court it must be assumed that it was never proved valid.

Laws of the 19th Century

As at the commencement of the previous century concerning the union of Scotland with England and Wales, on 1 January 1801 [2.39] Ireland joined the trio. The conglomerate was given the formal title of United Kingdom of Great Britain and Ireland and the Irish Parliament was dissolved.

George Rose's Marriage Act of 1812 [2.40] was officially called "*An Act for the better regulating and preserving Parish and other Registers of Births, Baptisms, Marriages and Burials in England*". It pointed out that improvements in the manner and form of keeping and preserving registers (of marriages etc. of His Majesty's subjects) would greatly facilitate the proof of pedigrees of persons claiming to be entitled to real or personal estate. It enacted that after 31 December 1812 new and separate register books of paper or parchment, provided by the King's printer for baptisms, marriages and burials solemnized according to the rites of the United Church of England and Ireland, should be used and kept in a dry, well-painted iron chest, either at the incumbent's residence in the parish or at the church. Unlike most other legislation regarding marriage, Rose's Act appears to have been adhered to in most places.

A schedule attached to the 1812 Act identified the information required in a marriage register, *viz*: name and parish of each party, when and where the marriage was performed, by whom, whether by banns or licence, and if parental consent had been necessary and given; to this were added the signatures of the married couple, two witnesses and the celebrant. Thus after 1812 you have an easier task when studying marriage registers. Copies on parchment of the marriages were to be sent annually to the bishop's registrar (so Bishops' Transcripts were confirmed by civil statute) together with lists of all registers then extant. The outcome of this nation-wide inventory of parish registers highlighted the appalling loss of original register books.

Whilst in 1753 Hardwicke had drawn attention to the publication of banns, as had canons of 300 years before, in many cases the veracity of the banns themselves (the information being published) was questionable. Thus in 1822 a Marriage Act [2.41] was introduced, effective from 1 September. This Act required signed affidavits, for which there was a 2s 6d fee, stating the Christian and surnames of both parties, whether of full age, their residences and how long they had lived there as occupiers or lodgers. Before reading the banns in a church or chapel, notice of these details was to be fixed to the main door and in some conspicuous place inside. The notices were to remain for the three Sundays while banns were read. After publication of banns the affidavits were to be given to the churchwardens for safekeeping in the parish chest. For these requirements to be enacted certain sections of Hardwicke's Act were simultaneously repealed.

If the couple planned to marry by licence an oath had to be sworn by both parties as to their own ages and how old they believed their partners were. If either party was under 21, unless a widow or widower, a certificate of approval from father, mother or guardian had to be furnished, countersigned by two or more witnesses; who, in turn, had to make an oath that they had also witnessed each other signing the document. If the parties were over 21 they had to supply copies of their baptismal entries from a parish register, signed by the incumbent and countersigned by a competent person. If certified copies could not be obtained for whatever reason (they had not been baptised, for example), a sworn declaration to this effect was required with an affidavit as to the age of the party, signed by someone who had known the individual for some time. Quakers and Jews and the Royal family were exempt from the Act, but anyone else who wished to marry by licence had to comply with its cumbersome requirements.

One result, particularly in the north of England, for the Act applied only in England and Wales, was for many couples to nip over the border to enjoy clandestine marriages in places such as Gretna and Annan in Scotland, where neither Hardwicke nor this Act applied. The other outcome was the Act being repealed in 1823 by two further Acts, but not before several months of documentation had accumulated - inconvenient at the time but a tiny Aladdin's Cave for us today. For marriages following the publication of banns, the sworn affidavits of names, ages and residences of the couple should today be with the parochial material in county record offices. For marriages by licence the fortunate researcher may discover copies of baptismal entries and sworn statements on age and residences of the parties, filed with the ecclesiastical court marriage licence documentation in diocesan archives, mostly also in county record offices. Marriage registers and their keeping were unaffected by the 1822 Act or indeed by its replacement by the 1823 Acts.

On 26 March 1823 [2.42] the 1822 requirement for affidavits was repealed, and then from 18 July 1823 the whole 1822 Act was repealed and replaced by another Marriage Act [2.43]. The July 1823 Act reduced the required time for residence to fifteen days; but no proof of the 15-day period was necessary to support the validity of a marriage by licence. This Act also specifically stated that no bond was needed before granting a licence; however, allegations were still required and most places appear to have complied with this. If the marriage did not take place within three months a new licence had to be obtained. The marriage had to be solemnized in the presence of two or more credible witnesses, and entered into a register book, indicating that it had been celebrated by licence and, if either party was under 21, that parental consent had been given - but see Chapter 3. Forging a marriage licence was a felony punishable by transportation for life; if a couple married under a forged or false licence and they both knew this, their marriage was void. It was also void if the licence was in order but the clergyman conducting the marriage ceremony was an impostor.

The July 1823 Act effectively reintroduced Hardwicke's requirements regarding Common Licences but with different conditions. It also re-enacted the legality of marrying by banns and the provision of a Banns Book. Furthermore, this Act confirmed the use of a marriage register "to preserve the evidence of marriages" and how entries should be made from 1 November 1823. Quakers and Jews were again exempt. The penalty for falsifying an entry was transportation for life. A copy of this Act was to be kept with the marriage register.

Lord Lyndhurst's Marriage Act of 1835, dealing with marriage within prohibited degrees, and tidying up important legitimacy issues, is described in Chapter 3. In August 1836, Lord Russell's *Act for Marriages in England* [2.44] (stipulating methods, also in Wales, for solemnizing marriage), and *An Act for Registering Births, Deaths and Marriages in England* [2.45] (stipulating methods, also in Wales, for registering these events), were passed on the same day. The civil registration of marriages, births and deaths, applied briefly but not very effectively from

1645 to 1660, was thus enforced again and a civil solemnization of marriage was offered as an alternative to a religious ceremony. It was intended that both 1836 Acts should come into force on 1 March 1837, but not all necessary arrangements had been put in place in time; thus on 24 February 1837 another Act [2.46] suspended operation of both 1836 Acts until 30 June 1837. Still there were teething problems and yet another Act was needed later in 1837 [2.47] to "Explain" the 1836 Acts.

The 1836 Registration Act provided for a complete civil register of births, deaths and marriages in England and Wales from 1 March 1837, later modified to be from 1 July 1837. The Act repealed sections of Rose's 1812 Act and the July 1823 Act relating to marriages. It provided for a Registrar General in a General Register Office (GRO) to lead a team of Superintendent Registrars in Register Offices across England and Wales. In the event the GRO was opened in London at Somerset House which, in 1973, moved to St Catherine's House and, in 1997, to the Family Records Centre, Myddleton Street, Islington. The Superintendent Registrars were responsible for areas largely identical to those of the new Poor Law Unions, established in 1834 [2.48]; in fact, it was recommended that the Clerks to the Guardians of the Unions should be appointed as Superintendent Registrars. If there was no Board of Guardians, the Act provided for the Poor Law Commissioners to set up a local system and make appointments. The Superintendent Registrars were to divide their areas into Registration Districts and appoint a Registrar of Births and Deaths for each District. All appointments were to be approved by the Registrar General. No mention was made in the Act of any Marriage Registrars, but the 1836 Marriage Act (see below) stated that the Superintendent Registrar of Births and Deaths was also to be the Superintendent Registrar of Marriages, and he was to appoint a suitable person, approved by the Guardians, as Registrar of Marriages.

The Act provided for the supply of a defined format and pagination of register books and strong iron boxes in which to store them, and it even stated how many locks and keys they should have, who should hold the keys and who should pay for what. Duplicate marriage registers and forms for certified copies were to be provided for the priest of every church and chapel licensed for marriages and for every Quaker Registering Officer and Jewish Synagogue Secretary. At every marriage ceremony in these places of worship entries were to be made in both of the registers, signed by the official, the bride and groom and two witnesses. Anyone making false statements would be subject to the same penalties as for perjury. Any celebrant not registering a marriage or carelessly looking after the register books or copies in his care, was to be fined £50. Wilful damage or deliberately entering false information was a felony. If an error to an entry was discovered within a month by the person making the registration, no fine was payable, and it could be corrected in the margin of the register and the copies, adding the date of correction, in the presence of the Superintendent Registrar and two other credible witnesses.

One of the duplicate registers was to be retained at the place of worship and the other, when full, was to be sent to the Superintendent Registrar. Certified copies of all entries were to be sent quarterly to the Superintendent Registrar. He, in turn, sent these copies (on "Quarterly Days of Transmission") of all births, deaths and marriages to the Registrar General with the numbers of each, for which 2d per entry was payable [which incidentally encouraged more than one Registrar to falsify a few entries to boost his income]. Custodians of the retained registers were to permit searches to be made at all reasonable times and copies to be provided. Prices were fixed at 1/- for a one-year search and 6d for each additional year and 2/6 for a copy certificate. Superintendent Registrars and the Registrar General were to produce indexes for the books in their offices. These could also be searched and certified copies provided for stated fees, the moneys at the GRO to be passed by the Treasury to the Bank of England [2.49]. It is now possible to apply for copy certificates by post [2.50].

The 1836 Marriage Act confirmed existing procedures within the established Anglican Church but introduced other features, taking advantage of the 1836 Registration Act. Legally certified places of worship, such as nonconformist chapels, could on application, be registered for marriages. The Marriage Act enabled a civil Superintendent Registrar to issue a Registrar's Certificate permitting a couple to marry in an Anglican Church, a Quaker Meeting House or Jewish Synagogue in England and Wales, so long as they stated the accepted declaration (given in the Act) in the presence of two or more credible witnesses. The Registrar's Certificate had a similar function to the Church's banns, as the couple intending to get married had to apply in person beforehand and provide details on themselves, i.e., their names, occupations, ages, that parental consent had been given if appropriate, marital status, addresses and where the planned wedding was to take place (the exact requirements were laid down in Schedule A to the Act). Details were entered in the Superintendent Registrar's Marriage Notice Book and the entry was available for 21 days for anyone to see, so enabling them to object in writing if they knew of any legal impediment to the marriage. If any objection (a forbidding or caveat) was found to be frivolous, costs and damages were liable. The Superintendent Registrar judged all objections, referring doubtful cases to the Registrar General, to whom the objector had a right of appeal.

If there was no forbidding, the Superintendent Registrar issued a Certificate, printed in black ink. This enabled the couple to get married within three months by taking the Certificate to their priest or other celebrant which gave him authority to conduct the marriage ceremony by the rites of their faith. If the couple wished to marry in England or Wales in a place of worship other than an Anglican Church, Quaker Meeting House or Jewish Synagogue, the Certificate authorised their minister to celebrate matrimony according to those rites, provided the building in which the nuptial ceremony took place was licensed for marriages. Conditions for procuring and cancelling this licence were specified in the Act. In some cases, including all nonconformist places of worship registered for marriage, a civil Marriage Registrar had also to be present at that part of the ceremony when the couple exchanged vows (made their contract).

A Superintendent Registrar was empowered by the 1836 Registration Act to also issue a Registrar's Certificate only 7 days after the couple's details had been entered in the Marriage Notice Book. This was effectively a Superintendent Registrar's Marriage Licence (the Certificate was printed in red ink and bore "Licence" as a watermark) and equated to a Bishop's Common or Ordinary Licence. The subsequent ceremony could take place in any building, apart from an Anglican church or chapel, in the Superintendent Registrar's District that he had licensed for marriages, including his own office. This offered a civil marriage ceremony for the first time since 1660. A Registrar General's Certificate, equivalent to the Church's Special Licence was not available until 1971 [2.51]. Marriage by licence also had to be within three months of its issue.

The Marriage Act identified fees that could be charged and confirmed that all marriages had to take place with open doors between 8am and 12 noon, apart from those following a Special Licence. Marriages celebrated in unlicensed places or otherwise than identified in the Act were void. The Act, similarly to the Registration Act, stipulated that Registrars were to give regular copies of marriage entries to their Superintendent Registrars who had to verify them. Anglican Diocesan Registrars were to send the Registrar General annual lists of churches and chapels in which marriages could be solemnized accordingly to the rites of their faith. The Registrar General was to print a list of all such chapels and places of worship, stating the county and Registration District in which each was situated, with names and addresses of Registrars, Deputy Registrars and Superintendent Registrars. Copies of this list were to be sent to every Registrar and Superintendent Registrar.

Anyone solemnizing marriage, other than in a Church of England or registered building, or without a Registrar, or within seven days (or 21 days) or after three months from notification, was guilty of felony, as was any Superintendent Registrar who issued certificates outside the prescribed time periods or who registered null and void marriages. Prosecutions had to be brought within three years of an offence.

As the 1836 and 1837 Marriage and Civil Registration Acts required a duplicate of the marriage register entry to be sent to the Registrar General in London, many parishes felt the need to also compile Bishops' Transcripts was unmerited, and from this date most Transcripts comprise only baptisms and burials. There was a £10 penalty for failing to send the civil copies to the Registrar General; what a pity a similar fine was not imposed on clergy who failed to send Bishops' Transcripts to the Diocesan Registrar in former and ensuing years.

An Act of 1840 [2.52] provided for marriages in a District near to where the couple lived, while the Marriage and Registration Act, 1856 [2.53] was introduced to amend some provisions of previous Marriage and Registration Acts. Again, it applied only in England and Wales, although some sections dealt specifically with cases where one of the couple lived in Ireland or Scotland. From 1 January 1857 Guardians of the Poor were no longer to be involved in civil registration and other small modifications were made. Schedules to the Act identified new formats in which some details were to be presented, for example, Notices of Marriage (required under the 1836 and 1840 Acts). For a marriage without a licence, the Notice was to state this and be displayed in the Superintendent Registrar's office; for a marriage with a licence the Notice was not to be displayed and some other conditions of the 1836 Act were changed slightly. In any case, if the couple lived in two different Superintendent Registrars' Districts, only one Superintendent Registrar had to be informed; the length of residence was needed of only the party in the District where the Notice was given. A Registrar could appoint a Deputy.

For a couple intending marriage without a licence, where one lived in Scotland, a certificate of proclamation of banns signed by the Session Clerk of the parish where the proclamation had been made, was to have the same validity as that of a Superintendent Registrar of an English District in terms of giving authority to conduct the marriage.

If one of the couple lived in Ireland, the procedures were to be the same (identified in the English 1836 Marriage Act) as if they lived in two different English Registration Districts: if length of residence in Ireland was more than a month, this fact could be stated in the Notice and was to be dealt with as prescribed in the 1844 and 1845 Irish Marriage Acts (see Chapter 7). Any marriages which had taken place in England since the first (1844) Irish Act, in which one of the couple was living in Ireland, were to be valid, providing both had lived in their respective Districts for at least seven days.

The marriage could be solemnized in a registered building only with the consent of the Minister or one of the trustees, owners, deacons etc; or in a registered Roman Catholic building only with the consent of its Officiating Minister; or in a church or chapel of the United Church of England and Ireland only with the consent of the Minister, and in any case only by a duly authorized clergyman of the United Church and only by its Forms and Ceremonies.

A couple wishing to add a religious ceremony was unable to do so at a Register Office although they could do this elsewhere, in conjunction with their priest. They were to hand him the Super-intendent Registrar's Certificate and pay any fee; he was then permitted to solemnize their marriage, but not record it in the parish register. He could celebrate their marriage in an Anglican building only if he was a minister of the United Church of England and Ireland. If the marriage was planned by licence, according to the 1840 Act in a registered building, in a District where neither of the couple resided, and they were not Quakers or Jews, the Superintendent Registrar who had been notified of their marriage plans could provide that licence; it had the same validity as one issued by the resident Superintendent Registrar. The couple were able to marry in their normal place of worship if it was a registered building less than two miles from the District where they had given notice of their plans, provided they had stated in the Notice which of them usually worshipped there.

After a marriage had been solemnized, its validity did not depend on proof regarding the actual residence or period of residence of either party, nor on any necessary legal consent nor on the registration of a building according to the 1836 Marriage Act nor that it was the usual place of worship for one party. False information was perjury and punishable as such. If a valid marriage was celebrated as a result of false certificates or information, the Attorney General or Solicitor General was able to confiscate anything acquired from such a marriage, following the principles in the July 1823 Act for under-age parties married by licence.

Acts in 1857 [2.54] and 1860 [2.55] recited details on calling banns and conducting marriages in extra-parochial places, while an Act in 1886 [2.56] further dealt with (beyond the 1856 Act) the validity of marriages where one person lived in Scotland. Another Act, later in 1886 [2.57], and applicable only in England and Wales, made the permitted hours 8am to 3pm - see Chapter 3.

After the 1898 Marriage Act [2.58] Roman Catholics and Nonconformists were not required to have a civil Registrar present at their weddings, providing these took place in buildings registered for that purpose and in the presence of a duly authorised person, normally the priest or minister.

Laws of the 20th Century

Under civil law, a man in England and Wales had not been able to legally marry his wife's sister since 1536, even after his wife had died; the same restriction had applied way before 1533 under ecclesiastical law because of the affinity restriction. During the 16th Century, as explained above, there was considerable debate whether a man marrying his widow's sister was lawful. Definitely from the 99th Canon of 1603, and published in the Prayer Book from 1662, it was quite clear that a marriage of a man to his widow's sister was void and all children of such a union were illegitimate. The same applied to a woman marrying her husband's brother, even long after her husband had died - that was illegal, the marriage was void, and all children of that union were bastards. Whilst this situation was abundantly clear, many couples ignored the law and many clergy overlooked it. Nevertheless, when it came to inheritance the unfortunate illegitimate offspring had no legal claims at all.

With the death of Queen Victoria, Victorian virtues also died and the influence of the Christian Church waned. Views on marital rights shifted from definitive Biblical and Canonical statements to an acceptance of different basic and commonplace standards. The Marriage Act of 1907 [2.59] removed wife's sister (and husband's brother) from the catalogue of prohibited relatives, provided the wife (or husband) had died - in other words a man could thereafter legally marry his deceased wife's sister (and a woman could legally marry her deceased husband's brother).

The 1921 Marriage Act [2.60] enabled a man to legally marry his deceased brother's widow, provided his brother had died. Likewise a woman was permitted to marry her deceased sister's widower. As these marriages from 1921 were valid, any resulting children from now onwards were legitimate and so entitled to a legal inheritance. The 1907 and 1921 Acts applied throughout the British Isles, although marriage with a deceased wife's sister was possible in the Channel Islands from 1899.

Children born to parents who had not undertaken a valid marriage, no matter how regular or irregular, were legally illegitimate, even if their biological mother and father were subsequently legally married. The 1926 Legitimacy Act [2.61] made a child of parents of a void marriage legitimate if, at the time of intercourse which resulted in the child, the parents believed they were legally married. The Legitimacy Act, 1959, modified the provisions slightly, requiring the father to be resident in England (or Wales) at the time of the child's birth.

Following a Select Committee report of 1929 (see Chapter 3 for details), comparing ages of consent for marriage with those for criminal cases, an Age of Marriage Act [2.62] was introduced. This made all marriages void from 10 May 1929 if either partner was under the age of 16, but provided for cases where a genuine mistake as to age had been made. Parental consent was needed if a party was of nonage, i.e., under 21 (under 18 from 1970 - see below).

The Marriage Act of 1931 [2.63] permitted valid marriages between a man and his deceased wife's niece or aunt and his deceased nephew's or uncle's widow. Also permitted were marriages between a woman and her deceased husband's nephew or uncle and her deceased niece's or aunt's widower. Thus more formerly forbidden relatives were removed from the list as fully explained in Appendix II.

The 1949 Marriage Act [2.64] confirmed the 1931 situation and carried the table of 60 prohibited relatives in the First Schedule of the Act. However a different order and more distinctive names were used such as father's mother and mother's mother (for grandmother), father's father's wife and mother's father's wife (for grandfather's wife) and wife's father's mother and wife's mother's mother (for wife's grandmother). Those relatives who had been identified in the 1907, 1921 and 1931 Marriage Acts were put into a separate table, indicating that they were prohibited if the affinity link was alive, but permitted if the link was deceased.

The slight amendments in 1954, 1958, 1970 and 1971 to the 1949 Act are not considered in this Cameo. But it should be noted that the 1958 Adoption Act [2.65] regarded adopters and their adoptees to be within prohibited degrees. By the 1960 Marriage Act [2.66] a divorce was deemed to be the same as a death for the purposes of degrees of impediment to marriage. The age below which parental consent is required was reduced to 18 in 1970 [2.67].

Further relaxations to prohibited affinity kinships were introduced in England, Wales and Scotland (not Northern Ireland) from 1 November 1986 [2.68] permitting marriages under specific conditions with certain in-laws. From that date a man was legally able to marry his former wife's mother (his mother-in-law), providing his wife and his wife's mother's husband (his father-in-law) had died (divorce was not sufficient) and both persons were over 21. A man was also able to marry his son's former wife (his daughter-in-law), providing both his son and his former wife (his son's mother) had died and both parties were over 21. A man could also marry his former wife's daughter (colloquially termed step-daughter) or granddaughter (whether his former wife was living or not) or the former wife of his father or grandfather (whether they were living or not), providing both persons were over 21 and the younger person before reaching the age of 18 had never lived in the same household as a child of the family of the older person. A man was also able to marry his former wife's grandmother or the former wife of his grandson (whether his former wife or grandson were living or not).

3. Truly Married ? - Interpreting the Laws

Validity

A marriage not meeting all the legal requirements in place at the time, regardless of pomp or ceremony, was and is invalid. For example, if an Act prescribes banns to be published, or a licence to be granted by an ecclesiastical or civil authority, or even register pages to be numbered or lined, and one or more of these details is ignored, the marriage may be void. Equally, a marriage at a forbidden time of the day or period of the year, in an unlicensed building or between persons under certain ages or living in certain Districts or of certain kinship could also be void, depending on contemporary legislation. The following definitions, adapted from the 1970 Law Commission Report [3.1], may be helpful:

A **valid marriage** has no legal defects and is binding on all parties. It can be terminated only by death or a decree of divorce acknowledging the valid marriage and then ending it.

A **void marriage** has never come into real existence because of some fundamental legal defect. No decree of nullity is needed if the parties wish to end the partnership as it has always (*ab initio*) been void.

A **voidable marriage** is valid unless and until it is annulled by a court at the instance of one spouse during the lifetime of both. After the death of one spouse the marriage is unimpeachable.

Although these definitions are not retrospective, similar principles applied before 1970. (Divorce is discussed in Chapter 9.) Thus to evaluate if a particular couple was truly married, it is imperative to consider statutes in place at the precise time of the marriage, and not copies of those statutes printed at a later date which often omitted, or included other, clauses varied by subsequent legislation. Relevant aspects affecting the validity of marriage are considered in the remainder of this chapter.

Banns

Ban is an Anglo-Saxon word meaning proclamation; thus publishing, reading or calling banns (also termed "askings" or "spurrings") is a public announcement of a couple's intention to marry; it gives an opportunity for anyone knowing any just reason or due cause why they should not be married, to forbid the banns (object to the proposed marriage). This concept was warmly supported by the Church from earliest times and banns were formerly published - see Chapter 4 for details - during a church service on three Sundays or Holy days prior to the planned wedding day. By 1603 the publication was regarded as so important that it was incorporated into Ecclesiastical Law (Canon 63) and a priest who did not publish banns on three occasions before a marriage was liable for three years' suspension. The style of words for banns appeared in the Book of Common Prayer and has remained largely unaltered since 1662. The 1836 legislation, offering marriage by a civil registrar, provided for a similar notification of intent to be published at the registrar's office.

Licences

An alternative to a public announcement of an intended marriage is to obtain a dispensation in the form of a Common or Ordinary Ecclesiastical Licence from a bishop or archbishop, or since 1837 a similar licence from a Superintendent Registrar (see Chapter 4 for details on licence procedures). A Special Licence can be obtained, in extreme circumstances, from the Faculty Office of the Archbishop of Canterbury, or since 1971 the Registrar General. For either type of marriage licence, certain conditions have to be met, and in general a licence is more expensive than banns. However, a licence ensures privacy of a couple's plans from nosey servants, tenants, neighbours, even parents, and the marriage can take place within hours of obtaining the licence; such haste may be convenient for a busy spouse, during times of war, or in anticipation of an imminent birth.

Verifying the Contract

Before 1837, and from the time that records are available, most couples in England and Wales who married appear to have done so after the publication of banns or the receipt of a marriage licence from an appropriate ecclesiastical court; which court was deemed appropriate is explained in the Chapmans Records Cameo *Ecclesiastical Courts, Their Officials & Their Records* [3.2]. At a Synod of Westminster, as early as 1200, Archbishop Walter had declared in Canon 11 that banns or a licence were essential before marriage. However, prior to the Parliamentarian Act of 1645 (replaced in 1660) or Lord Hardwicke's reminder in 1753, it is difficult to prove that banns had been read as there were almost no formal registers of banns before then. The four documents arising from the application for and granting of an ecclesiastical marriage licence, the allegation, bond, bishop's register entry and actual licence, are identified in Chapter 1.

But the 1645 and 1753 Acts actually introduced a complication as all that was required for a valid marriage until 1645 (and from 1660 to 1753) was a mutual exchange of vows - an agreement between the couple that they would henceforth remain faithful as husband and wife, and by inference there were also no legal impediments to their forthcoming partnership.

Problems arose, as only to be expected, when it was necessary to demonstrate, or worse to verify, that the mutual agreement had taken place. It was to satisfy the need for verification, for example in inheritance claims, that canonists conceived the doctrine of "possessory marriage": this was deemed to be constituted if one partner was able to find tangible evidence such as showing that an exchange of gifts (*arrae* or *arrabones*) had taken place, or by producing two "unexceptional" witnesses. But alas, this could be problematical if the witnesses had died in the meantime, taking their verbal testimony with them. It would have been far more useful to us as researchers today, if instead of the concept of a possessory marriage (being evidence for the Church, and publicity for the Crown), marriage records or registers had been introduced by the mediaeval church authorities.

Less ambiguous than attempting to demonstrate an indisputable possessory marriage, was to exchange vows "at the church porch" where passing parishioners could see the couple in the sunlight - the real origin of the phrase "Happy is the bride the sun shines on" - not summer weather. Another scenario was "in the face of the Church", before the congregation, or at a formal ceremony with witnesses signifying, in a register, their presence at the verbal contract. The concept thus arose of a clandestine (literally, in secret) marriage which could be perfectly valid, but in the absence of witnesses was difficult to prove. Concern had been expressed back in 1351 "that none of our subjects shall presume to celebrate clandestine marriages, where one or both of the contracting parties lie in a sick bed" [3.3]. Convocation (the Church's parliament) had heard arguments in 1460 [3.4] that marriages by licence were clandestine, as the general public often were unaware of such unions taking place.

A clandestine marriage should not be considered as a synonym for an irregular marriage, where certain conditions of residence, age or time of day or year are not met, whereas at a regular marriage such conditions are satisfied. Strictly, in a regular marriage everything was presumed to be complete and consummated in substance and ceremony; in an irregular marriage all was complete in substance but not in ceremony. Moreover, an irregular or a regular marriage could be valid or invalid and could also be clandestine. The legal experts had a field day or, more correctly, several field centuries. However, to the disquiet of professional lawyers in 1732, *"A Treatise of Feme Coverts"* [3.5] was published in English as a lay-person's (sadly poorly indexed) do-it-yourself guide to the convoluted matrimonial and inheritance laws; most surprisingly for the time, it was aimed specifically at a female readership. But formal documents were being published in Latin for the last time and from 1733 ordinary citizens could understand the pleadings in their own cases. At that time a valid marriage required neither ceremony, blessing, nor witnesses; and whilst the Church preferred an ecclesiastical environment, any children of such unions were considered legitimate.

A further complication arose in England and Wales after 1753 because Lord Hardwicke's Act had not specifically identified every detail needed in the paperwork for a valid marriage. The Act itself offered no guidance on enforcement; it was left to individual publishers to infer from the Statute what detail was necessary and then produce printed register books with blank spaces for each marriage entry. Accordingly, for biographical information on the subjects of your research, you are dependent upon which publisher, if any, the parish, archdeaconry or diocese selected in the 18th Century as their stationery suppliers [3.6]. For many years both ecclesiastical and civil lawyers attempted to unravel the confusion created by Hardwicke until most of his Act was repealed in 1823.

Commencement

For many a century the actual point at which a marriage commenced was unclear and neither the Christian Church nor the State would make a definitive statement on this. Possibilities were the betrothal, the espousal, the point during the ceremony when the celebrant declared the couple man and wife, and the sexual union - the physical consummation of the marriage.

Strictly, betrothal was a formal arrangement between the potential bridegroom and his bride's kinsfolk. If the contract was broken the Church courts ensured that money was repaid by the initiating party - if the groom initiated the breaking of the contract he lost the bride-price he had laid down; or he received back that price plus a third if the bride had caused the rift. If the girl refused the man to whom she had been betrothed, the Church allowed her parents the right to give her to another man. In the north of England and on the Isle of Man, a form of betrothal which persisted until the 19th Century was hand-fasting: two senior family members agreed that the heir of one should live with the daughter of another for a year and a day. If the girl became pregnant within that time the parties were declared married, if not the contract was considered at an end and each party was free to marry or hand-fast with another. Hand-fasting, agreed between Highland chiefs, was also practised in Scotland. A subsequent marriage ceremony was deemed unnecessary as hand-fasting was a formal contract, and hence off-spring were legitimate, although this was disputed under feudal law. Bundling is sometimes confused with hand-fasting, but bundling was a courtship custom, not a contractual arrangement, as explained in Chapter 8.

Betrothal did not always take place and abduction or marriage-by-capture was not unknown. Initial objections from the maiden to an abduction constituted a rape-marriage but if she colluded with her abductor it was considered an elopement; and if she acquiesced in subsequent sexual intercourse, it was believed that both parties consented to the union, and the Church, albeit reluctantly, accepted this as a valid marriage. In modern terminology this would be regarded as a "Common-Law Marriage" (some would say "married on the carpet and banns up the chimney"): there was no licensing or solemnization but there was a mutual exchange of words of present intent (in other words a verbal contract) and the subsequent adoption of a married life-style. This has legal validity in Scotland today (see Chapter 7).

An espousal was regarded as being at a similar point to a betrothal in terms of when a marriage was deemed to have commenced. Strictly, however, a betrothal is an agreement between the bridegroom and the bride's family, while an espousal is an agreement between the spouses themselves to become husband and wife. Although the ancient ceremonies of espousal or betrothal preceded the marriage ceremony, there appear to be no separate espousal or betrothal registers. However, there are examples at Boughton Monchelsea, Kent in 1630 and Wrenbury, Cheshire in 1610 [3.7] of espousals being separately recorded in a parish register.

On the other hand, records of betrothals or engagements have appeared in newspapers [3.8] since their first issue and continue to this day. The amounts of the dowries, effectively the brides' fortunes, were popularly published in local and national newspapers and periodicals from the 18th and throughout the 19th Centuries.

Oral engagements and promises to marry, which did not culminate in a marriage, could be the subject of legal action from the mid-17th Century [3.9]. Such a Breach of Promise action had to be substantiated by material evidence in support of the promise. If the man made no attempt to contact the woman for some years after promising to marry her, she would receive little in damages; if, however, he persisted in his affections but failed to marry her, the damages could be considerable, depending on her suitor's courtship behaviour. Such actions were impossible after 1970 (1981 in the Republic of Ireland) [3.10] but not uncommon in the early 20th Century; accounts may be found in contemporary newspapers.

Canon Law originally made it quite clear that no marriage had taken place until man and woman had become one flesh, as described in the Bible [3.11]. Accordingly, if following an espousal either party immediately entered into a sexual union with a third party (i.e. married that party) then the former espousal was dissolved. From the 12th Century two different types of espousal became recognized: an espousal of future words where both parties plighted their troth to each other (promised each other) to thereafter become husband and wife - "I will"; and an espousal of present words, where the parties took each other as husband and wife there and then - "I do". In the case of the former (I will) the marriage became a fact only when sexual union had taken place. The latter (I do) was in reality an actual marriage and was as effective as if it had already been a consummated union; it therefore created a permanent bond, not normally dissolved even if one party committed adultery or went through a ceremony of marriage and sexual union with a third party. This type of espousal could, however, be dissolved by papal dispensation or by one party taking up religion.

A later definition, comparable to those of regular and irregular marriages above, was that for espousal nothing was presumed to be complete or consummated either in substance or ceremony; although sexual intercourse, without a marriage ceremony, converted an espousal into an irregular marriage.

Marriage and sexual intercourse were synonymous terms when the former was deemed to begin at the latter, and both the Bible and the early Christian Church made no distinction between the two terms when defining degrees of impediment. Today, however, impediments to marriage are distinct from impediments to sexual intercourse; in the 1956 Sexual Offences Act [3.12] different kindred to those in Marriage Acts are identified.

From at least 1837 [3.13] in England most authorities have accepted that marriage begins at the point in the religious or civil ceremony at which the celebrating official pronounces the couple man and wife. Indeed, this is termed a "Ceremonialized Marriage" - requiring licensing and solemnization. Even so, in some cases brought before the courts, the lack of children was offered as evidence that a marriage had not been physically consummated and so had never really taken place. Today a childless marriage, whether by accident or design, is termed a "Companionate Marriage".

The point at which a "Proxy Marriage" begins is open to debate. In such a situation a third party is used as a representative of either the bride or the bridegroom who is unable to attend the ceremony by virtue of distance or compelling patriotism: military service or imprisonment, for example. Henry VIII married his fourth wife, Anne of Cleves, by proxy in 1540 and in 1673 James II (when Duke of York) married Mary of Modena this way. Charles I and George IV also celebrated proxy marriages. In many cases, when the couple's circumstances changed, a secondary or subsequent re-marriage took place - applauded by the Church.

Other instances of secondary marriages occurred soon after the Interregnum; several couples who were married by a magistrate at a civil ceremony (see Chapter 2) also went through a (legally unrequired) church ceremony at the Restoration. Occasionally a secondary marriage was needed when it was found, after the wedding, that for a valid marriage one of the conditions (normally of residence or age) had not been met. Hence another ceremony was required in an alternative venue or after the legal age had been attained. In these cases the marriage began at only the later, valid, ceremony as the first was a 'non-event'.

Sometimes a couple decided to undergo a secondary marriage by banns if their first was by Common Licence, although the second one was legally unnecessary as the marriage had begun at the first. Some Nonconformists and Roman Catholics after 1753 went through a marriage ceremony according to their own rites, and also through a ceremony according to the rites of the Established Church. Before 1837, apart from practising Quakers and Jews, only the latter was valid under civil law, as mentioned in Chapter 2, and the marriage legally began only at that point. Further instances of secondary marriage were the numerous couples whose families' opposition had driven them to an irregular, though possibly valid, marriage away from home, but who later married again in a home parish after their families had accepted their choice of partners.

Post-mortem paternity has only recently been feasible as modern technology enables the preservation of sperm in cryogenic banks beyond the death of a potential father. If marriage is assumed to take place at the sexual union, then Post-mortem Marriage must also be plausible.

However, such techniques were not available in former times, the major period covered by this Cameo, and thus further elaboration on such marriages is inappropriate here.

Impediments to Marriage

From Biblical times restrictions have been placed on who should be permitted to marry whom with regard to existing family relations, or one party being already or previously married, or being in Holy Orders. In the Book of Leviticus [3.14] in the Old Testament, Moses passed on the Law of God to the Israelites. Banned relationships were defined for them, even though some took place in Egypt and Canaan; the punishment for breaching any of these bans was death. The 1611 Authorized Version of the Bible refers to "nakedness being uncovered" while the 1970 New English Bible bluntly states "no man should approach a blood-relation for intercourse" and then identifies specific forbidden kindred.

Canon Law was developed from Moses's words, qualifying impediments to marriage as consanguinity (blood relations), affinity (related through an existing marriage) or one party being already married or in Holy Orders. These canonical impediments were adopted with varying amounts of enthusiasm by the secular authorities in the British Isles; for example, Scotland made incest a crime in 1567 although it did not become one in England or Wales until 1908 [3.15]. Incest formerly meant a marital or sexual relationship with any blood or in-law relative (not just a close family member, see below). Over the years the secular authorities modified the canonical degrees of impediment of consanguinity and affinity through a succession of marriage and related Acts, some of which are outlined in Chapter 2. The more significant prohibitions are tabulated in Appendix II. Alfred Huth, himself an authority on the subject, identified 172 books and papers [3.16] written between 1477 and 1878 alone on marriage between near kin.

From earliest times until 1835 a marriage within the prohibited degrees of consanguinity or affinity may have been voidable, but could be dissolved only by an ecclesiastical court. For centuries children of such unions never really knew how they stood; however, in 1835 Lord Lyndhurst introduced a Marriage Act [3.17] which clearly stated that any marriage, within the prohibited degrees of consanguinity or affinity, taking place after the passing of the Act was absolutely null and void. The 1835 Act (incidentally it did not apply in Scotland) also stated that from its enactment no marriages which had already been celebrated within the degrees of impediment could be annulled by any ecclesiastical court.

If a couple was married within the degrees of impediment, but they were both ignorant of their relationship at the time of their marriage, and it was solemnized with the rites of the Church after calling banns, their marriage was regarded as "putative" and not real. Pollock and Maitland elaborate on putative marriages and off-spring therefrom - see Bibliography. Today, some authorities use the term putative marriage to signify a marriage by perception.

Consanguinity

The position of consanguinity was addressed very early in the life of the Church in the British Isles. According to Bede's *Ecclesiastical History*, Augustine sought guidance from Rome in 601 on who could marry whom; probably because Christian marital requirements and the words of Moses were insufficiently attractive to the entrenched practices of heathen Britons. Pope Gregory replied [3.18] "A certain temporal law of the Roman Republic permits the children of a brother and a sister, or of two brothers, or two sisters, to marry; we have, however, learned by experience, that the off-spring of such a marriage cannot thrive; wherefore it necessarily follows, that the third or fourth generation may intermarry, but on no account the second". He went on to point out that it was forbidden for a man to marry his brother's wife, which had been the cause of John the Baptist being beheaded. Gregory was credited in 750 with having said [3.19] "We decree that every one shall abstain from marriage to the seventh generation". This was interpreted as being so long as they "know them to be akin". The Church's main fear was sanctioning incest.

At the 1215 Lateran Council a marriage within the fourth degree of consanguinity or affinity was pronounced null, although a papal dispensation was obtainable if one had authoritative or financial influence. Before then marriage within the seventh degree of consanguinity was forbidden; but if it was within the sixth or seventh degree it was merely sinful (*impedimentum impediens*), not illegal (*impedimentum dirimens*), the latter rendering the marriage void. There was, however, considerable perplexity calculatiing kinship degrees of consanguinity (and affinity - see below).

For the calculation, one way of using the ancient Roman (civil) Law was to count the steps between generations to the common ancestor of each partner and add them together; thus brother and sister were in the second degree, uncle and niece in the third, first cousins in the fourth, and second cousins in the sixth degree of consanguinity.

Confusingly, consanguinity was also interpreted from the point of view of a common ancestor, all the children being in the first degree and all grandchildren in the second. The canonists in the Roman Catholic Church developed the latter system so that for relations in different generations the longer lines were used in the calculation; thus a marriage between brother and sister had no degrees of consanguinity, between uncle and niece was in the first degree, and between first cousins was in the second degree.

However, the pre-Christian Germanic Law, being founded on inheritance of land, and on which feudal law was based and from which Canon Law was also derived, did not recognize any degree of consanguinity between parents and children, because inheritance was automatic within this family unit; so first cousins were in the first degree of consanguinity.

In the British Isles, generally, the ancient Roman civil law of consanguinity was accepted by most authorities. However, as described in Chapter 2, Henry VIII thoroughly confused all understanding of impediment to marriage. Luckily Archbishop Parker of Canterbury came to everybody's rescue and defined forbidden named kindred in 1563. The Parliamentary Acts during the Interregnum (see Chapter 2) also stated forbidden kinships, not altering those identified by Parker. In the 1662 *Book of Common Prayer*, Parker's list was published, originally quoting the Canon Law degree of each of the sixty prohibited relatives (incidentally all within the third degree of consanguinity and affinity). Later editions of the Prayer Book retained the same sixty relatives but the kinship degrees were not quoted. Copies of Parker's list were pinned up and were to be found in every parish church throughout the British Isles. Forbidden kindred were re-defined during the 20th Century, as described in Chapter 2 - see also the next section.

Affinity

Relationships of affinity were a natural Christian development from the belief that at sexual union husband and wife become one flesh. Archbishop Hubert in 1200, for example, had stated at a Council of Westminster [3.20] "Let not a man contract marriage with a relation of his former wife ...". Based on this belief the bride's sister is in the first degree of affinity to the bridegroom, and her first cousin is in the second degree, and so on within her blood relations; these are of the first genus of affinity. The husband of the bride's sister is in the first degree, but of the second genus of affinity, which is rather academic as the bridegroom would not normally want to marry him anyway. However, the sister of the husband of the bride's sister is also in the first degree but of the third genus of affinity to the bridegroom, which might be significant to him; but to his bride she is of only the second genus of affinity, again somewhat useless information when calculating potential marriage partners.

Before the 1215 Lateran Council marriages were forbidden within the seventh degree of affinity of the first genus, but only to the fourth degree of the second genus and the second degree of the third genus. After 1215, readers of this Cameo may be relieved to know, affinities of the second and third genus were disregarded. However, within the first genus, affinity relationships are still significant today. The prohibited consanguinity and affinity relationships were redefined from time to time, particularly in 1907 [3.21], 1921 [3.22] and 1931 [3.23], as described in Chapter 2 and shown in Appendix II; they were also clearly tabulated in a schedule to the 1949 Marriage Act [3.24] but modified by the Marriage (Enabling) Act of 1960 [3.25], by Section 3 of the 1975 Children Act [3.26] and by the 1986 Marriage Act [3.27].

Legal loop holes arose if there were no children of a matrimonial union: this could be interpreted that no sexual union had taken place and so there was strictly no real marriage - hence prohibitions respecting degrees of affinity could not be applied.

Spiritual affinity was also taken seriously because baptism was regarded as a new birth; hence Ecgbert, Archbishop of York, decreed in 750 that "If any man shall marry a nun, or his godmother....let him be accursed" [3.28]. Godparents or sponsors, often friends of the parents, agree at a baptism to share responsibility for the child's spiritual welfare. Archbishop Hubert reiterated in 1200, "let not a godson contract marriage with the daughter of the person who baptised him, or with the daughter of his sponsor, born before or after" [3.29]. A Provincial Council in Scotland went even further in 1225 in stating "We forbid marriage between those who stand sponsors for the same child; also between persons who have the same sponsors; also between the godchild and the godfather or godmother, or their child" [3.30]. Accordingly, the Church denied a godson marrying his godmother or her daughter, although there is no scriptural authority for this in the Book of Leviticus Chapters 18 or 20, nor in the New Testament.

Holy Orders

The phrase "You are a bastard for your father was a deacon" was frequently heard in the King's Court. There are voluminous amounts of correspondence from Church authorities in Rome and Britain, addressed to priests and monks; these letters span over 1000 years from 456 to the Reformation and beyond, chastising the clerics for taking wives or, in some cases, several wives.

Northumbrian priests in 950 were told in Canon 35 "If a priest shall desert his wife and marry another, let him be anathema" [3.31]; (see Chapmans Records Cameo on Ecclesiastical Courts [3.32] for a description of the anathematisation procedure). In England, John Russel, a preaching prior and priest, was summoned before Convocation in 1424 for having publicly pronounced at Stamford that "a monk might lie with a woman without committing mortal sin" [3.33]. The place of Convocation within the Church Court hierarchical system is also fully explained in the Cameo on Ecclesiastical Courts.

However, even the Vatican itself was not above reproach and some Popes led lives that would have pushed other news out of the tabloid press for several issues. Pope Innocent VIII (not the most suitable title), whose sex was at one time questioned, later became "the first Pope to acknowledge openly his illegitimate children and, setting aside all established usage, to load them with riches" [3.34]. He even hosted the wedding celebrations of one of his sons within the Vatican grounds. When Innocent VIII died in 1492 he was succeeded by 60 year-old Alexander VI who had three mistresses and at least seven children, some of whom were awarded Spanish dukedoms; one daughter was also married at the Vatican with monstrous pomp on 12 June 1493. But it was obviously not the ambience of the Vatican that influenced Alexander's life style; even when a cardinal in 1460 he had been admonished by Pius II for taking part in a twilight orgy lasting from 5pm to 10pm. It is no wonder that throughout Christendom not a few felt that some reformation was needed.

Space precludes further elaboration here, although it may be noted that those in Holy Orders in England were not permitted to marry until well over a decade following the Reformation; indeed, on 16 November 1521 [3.35] and again in 1534 [3.36] Henry VIII proclaimed that any priests who had "taken wives and married themselves contrary to the wholesome monitions of St Paul" without his permission, should not administer any sacrament and should be deprived of their office and privilege. Although the marriages of those in Holy Orders were legalised by a temporary Act [3.37] in 1549, their issue were not recognized until three years later when another Act [3.38] of Edward VI legitimated priests' children. Dismay was caused in 1553 by Queen Mary [3.39] who had both these Acts repealed; but under James I [3.40] in 1603 priests' marriages were re-regulated, and their children once again legitimated on a perpetual basis.

Royal Family

A quite different impediment to marriage was introduced in 1772 by the Royal Marriages Act [3.41]. No descendant of George II (except issue of princesses who marry into foreign families) may marry without the prior formal consent of the Sovereign. Any marriage coming within this Act and not conforming to its conditions is void. On the other hand descendants over the age of 25 who have given twelve months notice to the Privy Council may marry, unless both Houses of Parliament have positively expressed their disapproval. This Act is still in force.

Lunacy

The Church made no attempt to address the question of marriages of lunatics, although the *Treatise of Feme Coverts* (1732), referred to an earlier document stating "lunatics may not marry. But a person who is deaf and dumb, may contract matrimony; and so may an idiot, and it shall bind him" [3.42]. In legal terms an idiot had such a defective mind from birth that he could not guard himself against common physical dangers; a lunatic had some lucid moments, sometimes enjoying his senses, sometimes, not. The State, in 1742 [3.43] apparently for the first time, declared lunatic wedlock to be null and void. In 1811 [3.44] the Act was confirmed and extended to Ireland. A person under a frenzy was regarded as a lunatic for the purpose of the 1811 Act - which incidentally was repealed by the 1959 Mental Health Act [3.45].

Age

A valid marriage required the couple agreeing to the matrimonial contract. To understand the nature of their union they had to have reached an age of rational consent. From time immemorial it was accepted that a child of 7 could make a rational decision and so the age for matrimonial consent was fixed at 7 years. However, it was not until puberty, 12 for girls and 14 for boys, that fruitful union was possible. Thus Church Courts often regarded a marriage from 7 as "imperfect", although not absolutely void, until both parties had reached puberty; the marriage could then be consummated or, apparently, the couple also had the choice of rejecting the arrangements and having their marriage declared void. The age of consent for matrimonial purposes, 7 years, or even 12 and 14 years old, was inconsistent with the age of consent under Criminal Law, 16 years old; but this anomaly remained in England, Wales and Scotland until 1929 and in the Republic of Ireland until 1975.

In many cases it seems the lower age of 7 was disregarded even by the Church, which went only so far as to say that babes in arms should not be given in marriage, unless there was an urgent need such as the desire for peace, not only internationally but even between local disputing landowners. However, a Canon [3.46] emanating from the 1175 Council of Westminster stated: those "who espouse infants to each other in the cradle do nothing, unless they both consent when they arrive at the years of discretion"; the Canon reminded those involved that "where there is no mutual consent there is no marriage".

It would appear, however, that little heed was paid by some to the Canon, if the ecclesiastical court records for the Diocese of Chester in the 16th Century can be believed. Frederick Furnivall, in the late 19th Century, found cases of marriages of 8, 9, 10 and 11 year-olds and even some of 2 and 3 years old being married and their cases being brought before the Church Courts between 1561 and 1566; he was so astounded that he had abstracts from the court records published by the Early English Text Society in 1897 [3.47]. Furnivall's research epitomized considerable interest in early nuptials expressed in *Notes & Queries* in the 1880s: for example from 1831 to 1851, out of 11,058,376 marriages in England and Wales, 154 grooms were under 17 and 882 brides under 16 [3.48]. But this puts the numbers, and those quoted by Furnivall, in true context as discussed by Peter Laslett [3.49]; less than half of one percent of all marriages were in this age range, and strictly they were betrothals, though termed marriages at the time.

Canon 100 of 1603 forbade, but did not invalidate, marriage of persons under 21, except with parental consent. The legal age for marriage from 29 September 1653 (see Chapter 2) was fixed at 16 for a man and 14 for a woman, and any contract or marriage of persons below those ages was void. In 1660 the pre-Interregnum laws were reinstated and the ages of marriage reverted to 14 for a groom and 12 for a bride, and the age of consent returned to 7 years.

Lord Hardwicke's 1753 Marriage Act (see Chapter 2) also placed age constraints, making it illegal for those in England under the age of 21 to get married without the consent of their parents or guardians, as was the case in continental Europe. Incidentally in Scotland and America such parental consent remained unnecessary for a marriage to be valid. However, the consent requirement was repealed and replaced in 1823 [3.50]. The replacement Act directed that such consent be obtained, although a marriage wanting it was neither void nor voidable; however, any property of the nonage party did not pass to the elder party. In effect, therefore, from 1823 the ages at which a couple could undergo a valid marriage, even without parental consent, reverted to 14 for boys and 12 for girls; although some marriages of younger children still took place.

As mentioned in Chapter 2, The House of Lords was concerned in 1929 that Criminal Law fixed the age of consent at 16, while matrimonial cases regarded 7 as the age of consent. A Select Committee was set up [3.51], chaired by Lord Emle, and analyzed the 1,180,835 marriages recorded in England and Wales between 1924 and 1927. The evidence showed that of those marriages there were 119 cases of girls and only 4 of boys under 16. The committee concluded "that the moral sense of the people rejects marriage at, or approximate to, the legal minimum age". The resulting Age of Marriage Act [3.52] made all marriages void from 10 May 1929 if either partner was under the age of 16, although parental consent was still required for minors (persons of nonage). This was altered from 21 years to 18 years from 1970.

Another marital age constraint was the restriction placed on young people serving an apprenticeship. As the terms of many apprenticeships forbade marriage, most males under 24 until 1766, under 21 thereafter, and girls under 21, had to forfeit their apprenticeships if they married.

An old English proverb relating to the ages of matrimony, quoted by Burn [3.53] in 1829, may be worthy of preservation:

"The marriage of a young woman and a young man is of God's making, as Adam and Eve; of an old man and a young woman, of our Lady's making, as Mary and Joseph; but of an old woman and a young man, by the Author of Evil".

Place

If a valid marriage required only a mutual agreement between the spouses, this could obviously be arranged anywhere; even some form of Christian blessing by a priest could be performed in any place. Nevertheless, the Church, both before and after the Reformation, preferred the marriage ceremony to be conducted in a consecrated building [3.54], an abbey, cathedral, church or chapel. Marriages in taverns were certainly discouraged from 1220 by Richard, Bishop of Durham [3.55]. When the secular authorities began equating religion with politics and non-Anglicans with anti-royalists, one way of monitoring such groups was to license their places of worship. A rule-of-thumb method of regulating marriage was to combine the requirement for banns with that for a hallowed building, hence stipulating that for validity a marriage could take place only in a building licensed for the publication of banns. This arrangement applied to all marriages celebrated after the calling of banns or the granting of a Common Marriage Licence. A Special Licence granted by the Archbishop of Canterbury permitted, in theory as explained in Chapter 4, a marriage to be conducted anywhere, as specified on the licence.

Whilst this worked well in general, a few embarrassments were caused now and again on discovering that certain buildings, some well-known including St Paul's Cathedral in London, had never been licensed for banns publication although it had been assumed they were. Marriages conducted in such places were certainly void after Hardwicke's 1753 Act and resulting children illegitimate. A matrimonial case brought before the Court of the King's Bench in 1781, concerning a marriage in a chapel erected and consecrated in 1765, i.e. after Hardwicke, resulted in the marriage being declared null and void. As a direct consequence, another Act [3.56] was swiftly introduced whereby all marriages solemnized before August 1781, in any church or chapel consecrated since Hardwicke, were to be regarded as valid. Many similar Acts of Parliament (for example in 1804, 1808, 1818, 1819, 1822, 1824, 1825 [3.57] and 1831 [3.58]) were introduced to retrospectively validate marriages and legitimate any children.

The 1836 Marriage Act, as detailed in Chapter 2, not only enabled marriages to be solemnized at a Superintendent Registrar's office but permitted bishops to license chapels for marriages, for the convenience of couples who lived in remote areas and could not easily get to a parish church, or in highly populated areas where a single church could not meet the demand, provided certain conditions were fulfilled. Diocesan Registrars sent the Registrar General lists of licensed chapels in their dioceses belonging to the Church of England. In return the Registrar General published lists, which you may find useful, of registered places of worship and where they were situated.

The lawful places in the 19th Century where marriages could take place were identified [3.59] as:

a) In any place under a Special Licence of the Archbishop of Canterbury according to 4 Geo IV, c.76. [July 1823]
b) Generally in any parish church or in any licensed church or chapel.
c) In extra-parochial places, in certain cases.
d) Abroad: - when solemnized according to the local laws of a Christian State;
          - if solemnized according to 55 & 56 Vic c.23. [1892].
e) On board one of Her Majesty's ships on the high seas, by a lawful chaplain, according to 55 & 56 Vic, c.23 s.12.
f) Within the lines of the army in a foreign country by a lawful chaplain or any person officiating under the orders of the commanding officer, according to 55 & 56 Vic c.23 s.22.
g) In a registered building or at the office of a Registrar, under the Acts for marriages without religious ceremonies or with religious ceremonies other than those of the Church of England according to 6 & 7 Wm IV, c.85 [17 Aug 1836], as modified by 19 & 20 Vic, c.119 s.6. [29 July 1856].

More than a few religious sects after the Reformation, even after 1836, including the Roman Catholics who opposed the break from Rome and its Canon Law, and those Nonconformists who felt that the Protestant movement had not distanced itself far enough from Rome, refused to apply for licences for marriage at their places of worship. Accordingly any marriage rite that they celebrated was illegal and any children produced by a couple who believed they were united in this way were bastards - unless the couple also went through a marriage ceremony celebrated or presided over by a licensed official in a licensed or registered building.

Time

Certain times of the year and hours of the day were regarded by the Church as inappropriate for marriage; some periods were based on Christian principles, others adapted from pagan superstitions - see Chapter 8. In 364 the Church banned nuptials during Lent and by the 13th Century [3.60] forbade "any priest to celebrate a marriage from the beginning of Lent to the octaves of Easter". The following verse in the Beverley, Yorkshire parish register of November 1641 illustrates that the concept of forbidden seasons was not swept aside by the Reformation:

> When Advent comes do thou refraine,
> Till Hillary set thee free again;
> Next Septuagesima saith thee nay,
> But when Low Sunday comes thou may;
> Yet at Rogation thou must tarrie
> Till Trinitie shall bid thee marry.

Lyndwood, the 15th Century lawyer, interpreted that while a marriage contract could be drawn up, matrimony was not to be solemnized "from the first Sunday in Advent until the octave of Epiphany exclusive; and from Septuagesima Sunday to the first Sunday after Easter inclusive; and from the first Rogation day until the 7th day after Pentecost inclusive" [3.61]. "Marry in Lent, and you'll live to repent" was quipped, and so March weddings were unpopular whilst those in April (after Lent) were favoured. June was often chosen, not so much for the better weather but because the goddess Juno protected women and marriage. Winter weddings, after harvest, were chosen by many families, although December 28 (Childermas or Holy Innocents Day) was often avoided, being the commemoration of Herod's massacre of the children.

Regarding the day of the week, Sunday offered the best opportunity for publicity, so dispelling any suspicion of a clandestine union; Sunday also had the advantage that more parishioners could take a few hours from work to participate in the festivities, although the Puritans were strongly opposed to Sunday weddings (see below). The following old English rhyme is noteworthy:

> Monday for wealth,   Thursday for losses,
> Tuesday for health,   Friday for crosses,
> Wednesday best day of all,   Saturday no luck at all.

The time of day for marriage to take place was stipulated in a Canon of 1603 to be only between 8am and 12 noon, during Divine Service. This limitation ensured a public (and not clandestine) wedding and, equally important, couples were more likely to be sober then. The *Directory of Public Worship* (replacing the *Book of Common Prayer* from 1645 to 1660) removed most restrictions by stating "at some convenient hour of the day, at any time of the year, except on a day of publique Humiliation. And we advise that it be not on the Lord's day". Under the July 1823

Marriage Act it was a felony to marry other than between 8am and 12 noon unless by Special Licence. The 1886 Marriage Act [3.62] extended the hours for marriage after banns to between 8am and 3pm; Canon 102 was amended in 1888 to enable Common Licences to be granted for marriages between 8am and 3pm. In 1936, Canon 102 was amended again to enable marriages to be celebrated between 8am and 6pm. This was confirmed by Statute in 1949 [3.63]; Quakers and Jews were exempt from such constraints and a Special Licence (in theory - see Chapter 4) enabled a marriage to take place at any time or place. Revisions to Canon Law in 1959, 1964 and 1969 did not alter the legal hours of marriage in the Church of England. Even today, a person who solemnizes marriage outside the permitted hours can be imprisoned for up to 14 years.

Legitimating Bastards

"Once a bastard, always a bastard" may be said in frustration of one's boss today, but it is based on the reality that until 1926 in England and Wales, and 1931 in the Republic of Ireland, any children of a couple not validly married were illegitimate bastards, even if the parents later married. Even the Legitimacy Acts of those years, and amendment Acts subsequently, were very restrictive as to the conditions by which legitimation was possible. However, a number of practices were undertaken to reduce the stigma of bastardy and even ameliorate the lack of inheritance, and several Parliaments enacted Statutes hoping to deter parents from procreating illegitimate off-spring or "chance-children" or "chancelings" as they were often termed.

An Act in 1575 [3.64], in force until 1863 [3.65], and another in 1610 [3.66] enabled magistrates to send parents to the House of Correction if not supporting their illegitimate children. In exceptional circumstances a special Parliamentary Act or a bishop could provide legitimation if convinced that before the birth of the child the parents had been through a form of marriage which was invalid through a technical flaw, for example in the qualifications of the priest, or if the parents could demonstrate they were unaware of their existing consanguinity or affinity relationship; such wedlock was termed a "putative marriage".

In some parishes illegitimate children attended the subsequent church marriage of their parents and were given some form of blessing under the care-cloth or mantle (see Chapter 4) held over the bride and groom. They were, accordingly, termed "mantle children". Whilst not legally legitimating a child, this was acceptable by local custom as it provided some respectability to a public declaration of adoption by the real parents. However, formal and legal adoption was impossible in England and Wales until 1926 [3.67], in Northern Ireland until 1929, in Scotland until 1930 and in the Republic of Ireland until 1953 [3.68]. It was not until 1950 [3.69] that adopted children in England and Wales had the same rights as natural-born children. Unofficial adoptions had taken place long before the 20th Century, in many instances with legal deeds and formal surname changes, but in most cases the child had few legal rights.

4. Christian Marriage Rites & Records

The Christian Influence

Christianity added a sanctity to the civil status of marriage declaring it an ordinance of God. Prior to the Reformation, wedlock was the seventh sacrament [4.1]. Although a valid marriage in the British Isles did not require (see Chapter 3) a religious ceremony in the form of a nuptial blessing, the Church demanded certain standards from the mid-12th Century. A bride and groom who indulged in intercourse before the blessing of their marriage were guilty of sin and put to penance:

"On pain of excommunication we prohibit the espoused from having any carnal intercourse with each other before matrimony; otherwise let them come four times a year to the cathedral church and publicly undergo the discipline (i.e., the scourge) before the great (west) door, and also in the principal streets. On other fast days let them receive the discipline in their own parishes" [4.2].

The whole ecclesiastical procedure (outlined in Chapter 3) required an initial notification of the proposed marriage either through publishing banns or dispensing with this by procuring a Common or Special Licence; a fuller description is given below. This enabled objections to the union to be raised publicly, or the couple to affirm through the licence application process there were no canonical impediments to their marriage. Then followed the nuptial blessing, a series of ceremonies, which over the years became fused into one service, during which the couple were declared husband and wife. Following the marriage ceremony, from 1538, the clergyman entered a record of this into his marriage register, particularly after 1714 when it was proposed that there should be some indication if the marriage had been celebrated after the publication of banns or by licence. Some clerics simply wrote *lic* or *l* beside the entry. This addition was not always made and certainly many bishops' transcripts and other copies of marriage registers rarely note after which procedure the marriage had been celebrated.

The record of a marriage may appear in more than one place for a variety of reasons and at a casual glance could be misinterpreted as two or more distinct marriages. Careful scrutiny may reveal that the first entry is actually the record of a betrothal or espousal, or of the reading of banns, or of the payment of a tax or duty or fees connected with the marriage. There are also records of banns for marriages planned for other parishes and notes of marriages that have been solemnized elsewhere. Other examples of secondary marriages are referred to in Chapter 3. The multiple recording of a single event may not be appreciated until indexes are available of all licences, banns or register entries in published texts or in microfiche or CD-ROM editions.

Procedure by Banns

The practice of publishing banns became widespread throughout the western Church after Pope Innocent III ordered it at the 1215 Lateran Council - and this also held certain legal advantages over a marriage without banns, such as a putative marriage resulting in legitimacy and bastardy problems. There was also the financial advantage of marrying by banns compared with the rather expensive purchase of a licence. Archbishop Walter Reynold at Oxford, in 1322, reminded his clergy "before matrimony is contracted, let priests interrogate the people, under pain of excommunication, to declare any impediment which they may know by three public banns, on three Sundays or festivals distinct from each other" [4.3]. To this day the reading of banns on three successive Sundays continues to be the requirement for publication, which has some disadvantages: a public announcement from the pulpit of a couple's plans for marriage equates to the media scooping a story which the couple may well wish to keep a personal matter; furthermore, the time element can present difficulties for a soldier about to depart with his regiment, a merchant about to leave on a business trip, or possibly a couple who wish their child to be born in wedlock.

The banns were published, read or called in the parish church where the couple lived. If the bride and groom lived in different parishes they were read in each parish. In many churches, including Hope in Derbyshire and Croxton Kerrial in Leicestershire into the 19th Century, the Parish Clerk would immediately stand up and proclaim "God speed them well", to which the congregation responded "Amen". Traditionally banns were read immediately before the sentences for the offertory, but see below. During the Civil War, the requirement to call and record banns continued; the banns, termed "publications" at this time, could be called in the market place or the parish church. Throughout the three weeks required for publication, both before and after the Civil War, anyone could come forward and forbid the banns, in other words cite the impediment and hence the reason why the marriage should not go ahead. It was not uncommon prior to the New Poor Laws introduced in 1834, to object to the marriage of a poor couple who might become a drain on parish funds, as is apparent from some ecclesiastical court cases.

If the couple lived in separate parishes, the result of publishing the banns (a forbidding or not) was sent from one parish to the other. If there was no objection the couple was entitled to get married in either parish. It was customary in many parishes to interdict - not because there was truly an impediment but to cause comparative strangers to prove their credentials. Sometimes the marriage did not take place, even if there was no objection, presumably because of a change in circumstances for the groom or his intended bride, perhaps simply changing their minds.

The residential qualification was not always observed. If a marriage was solemnized elsewhere, albeit irregularly, it was regarded as being conducted in secret, and hence termed clandestine. As described in Chapter 2, the numbers of these clandestine marriages were escalated inadvertently by taxation Acts of Parliament at the close of the 17th Century. Lord Hardwicke's Act of 1753 attempted to clear up the growing confusion and malpractice in the application of banns and licences. From 25 March 1754 marriages in England and Wales had to be celebrated publicly by a properly qualified minister of the Established Church, in a lawful place of worship. In addition, due notice by the publication of banns or by licence, the certified consent of parents or guardians if the parties were under 21, and the proper keeping of formally witnessed records, were all made compulsory. Very many marriages which had taken place prior to this by no means met these criteria; as such they were classified by Hardwicke and his supporters as "Clandestine Marriages" although they were not conducted in secret and, as described above, many of these matrimonial unions, whilst irregular, were quite valid under the laws pertaining at the time.

However, in many instances banns had been properly published, although this fact was rarely recorded anywhere. Notable exceptions were from 1645 to 1660 during the Interregnum when more recorded banns (publications) seem to have survived than for any other period until 1753; in fact, during this period more banns records than actual marriage entries survive. The marriage ceremonies of Jews and Quakers, as a result of considerable lobbying by ardent supporters, were exempt from the provisions of the 1753 Act, as explained in Chapter 5. Also outside the Act was any marriage solemnized beyond the seas or in Scotland, where the equivalent of Hardwicke was not introduced until 1940, as explained in Chapter 7.

Hardwicke required the publication of banns to be in a church or chapel previously licensed for this purpose and after the second, although this requirement appears to have been printed only in the 1809 Oxford Prayer Book. lesson. (Prior to Hardwicke's Act banns had been read immed-iately before the sentences for the offertory). The July 1823 Act confirmed banns should be called after the second lesson; in Ireland they were published after the Nicene Creed. Banns read in a church not licensed for their publication were regarded as unpublished; hence any subsequent marriage should be invalid (although Acts [4.4] in 1804, 1808, 1818, 1819, 1822, 1824 and 1825, and many later years, mostly associated with church buildings, were introduced to cover this situation). If there was no objection the couple was entitled to get married in one parish or the other, either at the parish church or in a licensed chapel in either parish. The 1823 Act [4.5] emphasised the compulsion to marry at one of those venues "and in no other place whatsoever".

If false names were deliberately used when reading the banns of their proposed marriage it was deemed that the banns had not been published, which often caused legal problems with the subsequent marriage. The first secular case [4.6] brought up (in 1785) after the introduction of Lord Hardwicke's Act judged that as false names had been published the banns had not been read. Using a false name, rather than procuring a licence or even entering a clandestine marriage, may have been prompted in some cases if the actual surname had embarrassing connotations.

Some sections of Hardwicke's Act were repealed in 1794 and 1822 but the July 1823 Act effectively reintroduced Hardwicke's requirements, with different conditions regarding Common Licences. It also re-enacted the legality of marrying by banns and the provision of a Banns Book. The 1836 Acts confirmed the legal requirement for formal notification of a proposed marriage by giving notice to a civil registrar, and for religious purposes either by publishing banns, or by obtaining an ecclesiastical licence. With slight modifications this is still the case today.

Banns Records

The publication of banns, particularly but not exclusively after Lord Hardwicke's Act, was recorded either in the marriage register or in a separate Banns Book, in some instances called a "Notices Book" as the banns were interpreted as giving notice of the intention to marry. The Banns (or Notices) Book may have information additional to that given in the marriage register and usually more than given in the Bishop's Transcript. For example, in the Banns Book occasionally there are the names and addresses of the parents if the couple were minors, the addresses of both parties and their marital status - particularly useful if the bride was a widow, a fact not always apparent from a marriage register. Strictly a Marriage Notice Book was the civil ledger in which intentions to marry were entered after 1 July 1837; these were copies of the notifications to a Superintendent Registrar of impending marriages. Under the 1836 Marriage Act [4.7] such books were to be open at all reasonable times for free inspection, although the Registrar was entitled to a fee of one shilling for every copy of an entry.

Procedure by Licence

Before 1837 the recognized method of marrying without banns was by means of papal dispensation (until 1534) by issuing, at a price, an ecclesiastical licence. Canon Law provided for the granting of a Common Licence for the solemnization of matrimony by an archbishop, a bishop or an ordinary [4.8] and this was confirmed in 1534 by temporal statute [4.9]. The same Canon further stated that "no licence shall be granted but unto persons only as be of good state and quality" and "no licence shall be granted but upon good caution and security taken"; this security was explained in Canon 102 of 1603, annulled in 1753. Licences were abolished during the Interregnum. Proposals for matrimonial licences were debated in the Lower House of Convocation [4.10] during the reign of Queen Anne in 1712 and Canon 102 was redrafted in 1714 [4.11] requiring register entries to differentiate between marriages after licences and marriages after banns. In practice, persons who could afford a licence were often those "of good state and quality" anyway, although even small landowners or professionals, as well as the gentry, took advantage of this method of marrying without the publicity or the delays necessitated by calling banns.

In 1808 [4.12] a Stamp Duty was imposed on the licence itself, whether it was written or printed on skin, vellum, parchment or paper. Special Licences attracted a higher duty (£4) than Common Licences (10s.). In 1815 [4.13] the duty on a Special Licence was increased to £25.

The ecclesiastical administrative system for issuing a Common Marriage Licence, from which church court and why that court, was very similar to that for granting probate. If both parties lived in the same or even different parishes but in the same archdeaconry an archdeacon's licence was issued. If the parties were from parishes in different archdeaconries but within the same diocese, a bishop's licence was issued from a Consistory Court, often by the Diocesan Chancellor or a Surrogate in the diocese acting on behalf of the bishop. If the parties were from parishes in different dioceses but in the same province the licence was issued by either the Archbishop of Canterbury through his Vicar General or by the Archbishop of York, or their Surrogates, depending on where the parties lived. If the parties were from different provinces the licence was issued by the Master of Faculties from the Faculty Office of the Archbishop of Canterbury. Certain parishes were outside the control of the ecclesiastical courts as regards licences, and in some cases also for the granting of probate. These special or 'peculiar' parishes were permitted to issue their own marriage licences, although an Archbishop in certain peculiars was able to act as an Ordinary to issue a licence.

If planning to marry by Ordinary (Common) Licence, normally the groom, with a colleague or relation, went to see the presiding ecclesiastical officer of the marriage licence court - the archdeacon, the chancellor etc. or a surrogate. Some surrogates sold bogus blank licences. An allegation (a statement made on oath, the legal term being an affidavit), was made by the groom to the cleric of his intention to marry by licence, that there was no lawful impediment to the marriage and that canon law was not being infringed. Occasionally the bride, or even the colleague or relation without the groom, made the preliminary visit and swore the allegation. From 1753, if either the bride or the groom was under 21, it was a statutory requirement to obtain the written permission of parents or guardians (this was obtained before 1753 in many instances); this was handed over to the cleric when making the allegation.

In the case of the allegation being made in an archdeacon's court, or before a surrogate, the written allegation was forwarded to the appropriate diocesan registrar for filing. If either party was also an orphan, a copy of the Order in Chancery appointing a guardian was also attached to the allegation. Usually an allegation bears the date, names of both parties, their ages and marital statuses. If under 21, parental consent is indicated. Occasionally their occupations and addresses, but often only of the groom, are given. There may also be details of a previous marriage: if that had resulted in a divorce there may even be a copy of the associated Private Act of Parliament.

As a precaution against the allegation being untrue the groom was required to stand surety or was bonded, in a fairly large sum of money, jointly with his colleague or relation that the allegation was correct. A bond contains the obligations (often in Latin, until 1733) of the bondsmen with their names, addresses and occupations and the conditions of the bond, and (in English) the names of the couple and their ages if minors and the intended church or churches chosen for the marriage. This procedure was sometimes circumvented, or even violated, by the participating parties; one bondsman could be fictitious and a name and signature such as John Doe written in. Using Latin to describe occupations created some anomalies, for example, *"agricola"* applied equally to farmer, yeoman and husbandman. Although the 1823 Act still required allegations, bonds were no longer necessary; in a number of courts, however, bonds continued to be filed with the allegations.

In some ecclesiastical courts information from the allegation and the bond was entered in a separate Marriage Licence Register or Act Book; this is obviously useful for research today if the allegation and the bond have since disappeared. Some of these books have been calendared (sorted under the initial letter of the surname) - often of the groom only - into ledgers which are accordingly called Marriage Licence Calendars. Allegations made before archdeacons or surrogates were not always sent to diocesan registries and are now missing.

Canon 102 of 1603, already mentioned, stated that a marriage by licence should take place in the parish where one party lived, but this was rarely adhered to, even though it was reviewed in 1714. It was the practice in some areas for the couple, obviously having just collected their licence, to be married in the diocesan cathedral. However, Lord Hardwicke's Act required that at the time of the licence being issued one of the parties had to be resident in the diocese of the licensor and the marriage also had to take place in that diocese. Canon 102 was resurrected so that the solemnization of matrimony had to take place in the parish church or public chapel belonging to the parish where one of the parties lived for four weeks immediately before the granting of the licence; if one of the parties lived in an extra-parochial place, without a church or chapel where banns could be published, marriage should take place only in an adjoining parish.

The 1836 Marriage Act enabled a (Common) marriage licence or certificate to be obtained from a civil Superintendent Registrar after giving him notice; this was recorded in a Notices Book which was available for public perusal. This allowed a marriage to be solemnized by a parson in any place where prior to the Act marriages could have taken place following the publication of banns. The giving of notice to the registrar was deemed equivalent to the publication of banns.

The Archbishop of Canterbury was enabled by the 1534 statute to issue a Special Licence whereby the parties could marry at any time and place, consecrated or not; the statute actually gave the Archbishop the same power to grant faculties, dispensations and licences as the Pope had hitherto. The Archbishop of Armagh later similarly issued Special Licences in Ireland (see Chapter 7). The Bishop of Sodor and Man appears to have been given, or perhaps assumed, the power to grant Special Licences on the Isle of Man [4.14]. The conditions of each Special

Licence were specified within the licence which was issued on behalf of the Archbishop by the Faculty Office to the officiating cleric. This procedure was endorsed by Lord Hardwicke's Act and the July 1823 Statute that also addressed Common Licences. Prior to 1755 both the Vicar General and the Master of Faculties were able to grant Special Licences, but after 20 January 1755 only the latter issued them.

Very few Special Licences were issued prior to the 20th Century - in fact 99% of all marriage licences issued before 1900 were Common Licences. In a number of cases the residential requirement was fulfilled merely temporarily or even only on paper to (just about) meet the requirements. There was, nevertheless, a rise from eleven Special Licences in 1747 to fifty in 1757, probably as a result of Hardwicke emphasising that under a Common Licence a couple should marry only within the parish of one of them. Such a five-fold increase, albeit to an extremely low absolute number, caused Archbishop Secker to panic in 1759 and issue some guidelines whereby only Peers, Privy Councillors, Members of Parliament, barons and knights should be married with Special Licences. He also expected couples to marry within the normal canonical hours! Special Licences were also intended for a couple to marry in a place with which they had a real attachment, not a mere fascination.

Licence Records

The documentation associated with becoming married by licence has been identified above as the allegation, the bond, the marriage licence act book or calendar, the licence and the marriage register entry. The licence itself was issued by the bishops's or archbishop's court official to the bridegroom who presented it to the celebrant when he conducted the solemnization rite. In a few cases the licence was retained by the parson who put it in the parish chest - and thus it may now be with the parochial archives in the local record office. In other cases licences were returned to the diocesan registries for filing with the allegations and bonds (in some instances unfortunately misfiled as the licences were forwarded many months or years after the event). In yet other cases a licence was given to the couple on their wedding day who may have kept it within the family. If the licence was issued from a peculiar it could be anywhere today.

Some 20,000 original licences (1707-1892) from 24 London parishes were acquired in the early 20th Century by F A Crisp; abstracts of these are at the Institute of Historical Research, London. Copies of, and indexes to, the abstracts are held by the Society of Genealogists. Many of the original licences are now at the Institute of Heraldic and Genealogical Studies, Canterbury, some are with the Society of Genealogists which can advise on the holdings. As already explained, the Faculty Office was able to issue a Common Licence, on behalf of the Archbishop of Canterbury, for a marriage to take place in any parish in England and Wales where one party lived; its records from 1543 have been calendared and are now at Lambeth Palace Library [4.15].

The records associated with the Archbishop of Canterbury's Vicar General, issuing Common Marriage Licences within the Province of Canterbury, are also held at Lambeth Palace, in fact bound with those of the Faculty Office for Special Licences. The Vicar General's bonds begin in 1666 and those for the Faculty Office run from 1694 to 1823 (after when they were no longer necessary). Some of the Faculty Office marriage licence records have been somewhat inconsistently abstracted and indexes have been variously published by individuals and the Harleian Society (Vol 24) and the British Record Society (Vol 33). These volumes are available in many public libraries in the British Isles and in university and genealogical libraries throughout the English-speaking world. Manuscript calendars of others by surnames are available at Lambeth Palace Library; the Society of Genealogists has microfilm copies of some of these. The Vicar General's marriage licence records begin in 1660 and have been published to 1694 by the Harleian Society (Vols 23 and 30 to 34). Typescript indexes to 1709 and manuscript calendars to 1850 are in Lambeth Palace Library; the Society of Genealogists holds indexes to some of these. Harvester Microform [4.16] sells microfiche indexes of all Faculty Office and Vicar-General's licences. The National Library of Wales has a card index to Welsh diocesan licence bonds.

The Archbishop of York granted marriage licences for the Diocese of York and for the remainder of the Province of York when more than one jurisdiction was involved. Surviving marriage bonds, allegations and registered copies of licences are held at the Borthwick Institute [4.17]. York diocesan bonds and allegations survive from 1660 to 1950 and are filed together. Many allegations are hand-written on the bonds until 1733, after when they are separate documents; the bonds cease in 1823. Indexes to these have been published to date for 1735-49, 1750-65, 1765-79 and in ten-yearly volumes thereafter to 1839. The registers of diocesan licences disappeared during the 19th Century (except that for 1618-20 which survives). However, William Paver had previously abstracted notes for the periods 1567-1644 and 1660-1714; his notes have been published in the Yorkshire Archaeological Society Records Series Vols 7-20 (with a consolidated index in the Extra Series, Vol 2), 40, 43 and 46. Marriage bonds and allegations for some Yorkshire peculiars (notably that of the Dean and Chapter of York, indexed) are also in the Borthwick Institute, others are in Leeds [4.18]. The marriage licences for the Archdeaconries of Richmond and of Nottingham are held in Leeds and Nottingham [4.19] respectively.

Many county antiquarian, record and historical societies have also published material associated with marriage licences. In some instances the allegations have been used as the source of information, in others, the bonds, the entries in the Act Books or Calendars or combinations of these, together with remarks from the parish marriage registers. It is important that you know the sources from which such publications have been drawn; having found an entry in one of the indexes further research in the original documents or microfilm copies of them is strongly recommended. An excellent digest of what is held where and by whom is given by Jeremy Gibson in *"Bishops' Transcripts and Marriage Licences - A Guide to their Location"* [4.20].

Marriages licences for Scotland and Ireland and their whereabouts are described in Chapter 7. Licences for the Channel Islands are with the Ecclesiastical Courts' Greffiers; the few that are known to survive for the Isle of Man are in the Manx Museum Library [4.21].

The Marriage Rite

The first full description of the actual rite in the Christian Church is given in Pope Nicholas I's response at his conference with the Bulgarians in 866: the espousal took place first; then the bridegroom gave the ring to the bride, and the dowry, as a written document, was handed over in front of witnesses. The couple, who really from the espousal were married (see Chapter 3), then celebrated Mass; they were given a nuptial benediction (which is why the groom was called a benedict in those days) after the consecration (of the bread and wine) but before the fraction (breaking of the bread) while a pallium (cloth or veil) was held over their heads. (A later practice was for the bride only to be blessed.) As they left the church they were crowned. The crowns were afterwards hung up in the church ready for the next couple. This rite appears to be a direct adoption of the old Pagan Roman marriage rite, with the Mass substituted for the Sacrifice [4.22].

The *Treatise of Feme Coverts* contains a blunt description [4.23] of marriage before the time of Pope Innocent III (1198-1216): "The man came to the house where the woman resided, and in the presence of her friends and relations, took the woman to his own house; and this was all the ceremony". Presumably the friends and relations would verify that the couple had agreed their partnership. The husband was called a "baron", his wife a "feme".

Prior to the Reformation all Church rites were contained in five separate books: the *Breviary*, the *Missal*, the *Manual*, the *Pontifical* and the *Processional*. Solemnization of Matrimony was in the *Manual* (also termed the *Ritual*, the *Agenda* or the *Sacerdotal*). Different dioceses had slight differences in the prayers used, but by the 15th Century the Sarum Diocesan books were used in most of England, Wales and Ireland; for confirmation in 1543, Convocation imposed the *Sarum Breviary* throughout the Province of Canterbury [4.24].

Following the Reformation all the services in the Established Church were revised. On Henry VIII's death the boy King Edward VI ascended the throne with Somerset as Protector and Cranmer as the real reformer, not always behind the scenes; it was probably Cranmer who drew up the first *Book of Common Prayer*, placed before Parliament in 1548. This resulted in the first Act of Uniformity [4.25] requiring by 9 June 1549 the exclusive use of *The Booke of Common prayer and administracion of the Sacramentes and other rites and ceremonies of the Churche: after the use of the Churche of England*. The 'Forme of Solemnization of Matrimonie' in this Prayer Book was a slight variation from that in the Sarum and Hereford Diocesan books:

The opening address refers to the institution and dignity of marriage (reproaching the carnival wedding day that was actually enjoyed); the challenge to the bride and groom is quite specific. The ring is placed on the left (not the right, as in the pre-Reformation rite) hand and the two blessings of the ring are replaced by a single prayer for the couple. The statement "those whom God hath joined..." (of Lutheran origin) appears for the first time. The espousals are no longer at the door or porch but in the body of the church and there is no mention of the pallium. The nuptial blessing once more includes both bride and groom. The blessing is moved to before the Mass which is to be that of the day (not of the Holy Trinity). A sermon, in English, on married life is to be based on Holy Scripture. There is no reference to crowns used at the end of the ceremony.

After Somerset had been sent to the Tower of London it was feared that the new Prayer Book would be ignored and so in December 1549 the Anglican Church ordered all Breviary, Missal, Manual, Pontifical and Processional books to be called in and destroyed; this was confirmed by a temporal Statute [4.26]. Over the next three years a number of European reformers came to England and other service books were made available incorporating their influences, culminating in the *Second Book of Common Prayer*, published in 1552. Whilst there were many changes to prayers, to divine service and some sacraments, the marriage rite was untouched. However, Edward died on 6 July 1553. When he was buried by Cranmer on 8 August it was according to the new English rite, but simultaneously in front of Catholic Queen Mary, Gardiner said a Requiem Mass in Latin. By December the first Act of Repeal [4.27] was in force and administration of the sacraments "as in the last year" of Henry VIII was reinstated. But within five years a Protestant Sovereign was back: when Elizabeth I came to the throne in 1558 she initially restored the 1552 Prayer Book.

The *Book of Common Prayer* was withdrawn by the Parliamentarians [4.28] by statute in 1645 (see Chapter 2) and replaced by the *Directory of Public Worship*. Whilst the form for the marriage rite in the Prayer Book remained valid, incumbents who did not follow the new one printed in the Act and Directory were fined £5.

The nuptial blessing by a priest was replaced, by a further statute [4.29] of Oliver Cromwell in 1653, with a civil marriage ceremony to be performed by a magistrate; and it applied to Ireland as well as England and Wales. The use of a ring was forbidden and no other form of marriage was to be contemplated. The elected Parish-Register (Registrar) recorded the marriages (and births etc.), as described in Chapter 2; you should note that if the incumbent had been elected as the Register he could not solemnize matrimony, only a magistrate could do that, but the incumbent could record the marriage in the register book. The Register also organised the issue of certificates to confirm that the publication of banns, between the hours of 11am and 2pm, had taken place on three successive Sundays after service, or on three successive market days in the market place. In those parishes where this Act was complied with the records were extremely well kept.

The 1653 Act was confirmed on 26 June 1657 but superseded in 1660 after the restoration of the Monarchy by those laws in place before the Commonwealth. The legality of marriages by civil ceremony from 1653 to 1660 caused such concern that an Act of 1660 [4.30] was needed to confirm that they and all those contracted irregularly since 1 May 1642 were perfectly legal.

The calling of banns in the 1662 Prayer Book Service follows the principles of Pope Nicholas (866), mentioned above; an English reference of 1200, states that banns were to be called at Mass "when the greater number of people should be present" [4.31]. In the *Book of Common Prayer*, at the close of the first prayer of the marriage service, the following words appear "Therefore if any [person] can shew any just cause, why they may not lawfully be joined together, let him now speak, or else hereafter for ever hold his peace". Recital of these words, in effect, amounts to a fourth publication of banns.

The essential, legal, part of the Christian Marriage Rite, as practised today, is the solemn declaration made by the bride and groom, which has hardly varied from the centuries-old commitment of each spouse to the other. At some time during the ceremony the following words must be said by both the bridegroom and bride in the presence of the celebrant and witnesses:

> "I do solemnly declare that I know not of any lawful impediment why I, [Thomas Chapman], may not be joined in matrimony to [Mary Jones]".

Each must also say to the other:

> "I call upon these persons here present to witness that I, [Thomas Chapman], do take thee, [Mary Jones], to be my lawful wedded wife [or husband]"

In the presence of an authorized person, without a registrar being present, the words can be: "I, [Thomas Chapman], do take thee, [Mary Jones], to be my wedded wife [or husband]". Other words, such as honouring or obeying, may be added, according to the customs or traditions of the faith of the couple and the requirements of the celebrant. A couple who did not follow all the essential parts of the service were said to be "half-married".

Marriage Rite Records

The marriage itself, the solemnization of matrimony, within the marriage rite was recorded, with varying quality, in parish registers from 1538. These records are fully described in Chapters 1, 2, 4 and 5, thus only an outline is included here. It may be noted that following Hardwicke's Act, some of the instructions, provided by the printers, refer to each entry as a "Marriage Register". From 1597 copies of parish register entries should have been sent through the local archdeacon to the appropriate diocesan registry; these copies are termed Bishops' (in some cases Archdeacons' or Parish Register) Transcripts. These records are now in county or diocesan archives.

Registers of the Chapels Royal until 1858 are in RG8 at the PRO. Jewish, Quaker, Nonconformist and Roman Catholic marriages may be noted in their own registers or those of the Established Church (see Chapter 5). Many non-Anglican registers were deposited with the Registrar General in 1840 and 1858 [4.32]; some are in county record offices, others are with denominational historical societies or still in use at the local places of worship. Many non-Anglican registers have been transcribed, indexed and published. Transcripts of some registers of all denominations are on the Internet on the UK and Ireland genealogy pages HTTP: // MIDAS.AC.UK/GENUKI / .

From 1 July 1837 civil registrars have been responsible for recording every marriage in England and Wales and also able to solemnize marriage at a secular ceremony. As a consequence most Bishops' Transcripts of marriages cease around this date. Copies of the civil certificates are held by local Registrars and also by the Registrar General. National indexes to the Registrar General's copies may be consulted at Myddleton Place, London. Copy certificates may be purchased [4.33]. Microform copies of these indexes are available in many private and public libraries and similar collections. Registers of Authorized Persons (1899-1921) are in RG 42 series at the PRO.

Copies of many marriage registers are available from county archives in microform. Some registers have been partially or fully transcribed, indexed and published in book form by county parish register societies and similar historical records and antiquarian groups. Abstracts of marriage entries from either Parish Registers or Bishops' Transcripts have been taken, indexed and published since the late 19th Century by W P W Phillimore, Percival Boyd, and very many other individuals and organisations. Some of these works are available only locally or in specialist libraries, such as that of the Society of Genealogists, others published their results more widely but even then in limited numbers; but they did not always indicate their precise sources. The Institute of Heraldic & Genealogical Studies [4.34] houses the Pallot index of marriages solemnized from c.1780 to 1837 in very many London churches and chapels. County archives can advise you what is available for their locality; the holders of many private and society indexes may be found in "Marriage, Census & Other Indexes" by JSW Gibson and E Hampson [4.35].

Individuals named in most marriage indexes and copies are only the bride and groom. However, there is at least one on-going index to witnesses of marriages in England, Wales, Scotland and Northern Ireland [4.36]. For very many years, members of the Church of Jesus Christ of Latter Day Saints (Mormons) have been copying partial or full entries of marriages (and baptisms) from registers and other sources of all denominations in every part of the British Isles. From the copies alphabetical indexes of the names of brides and grooms have been published by counties in the International Genealogical Index (IGI) in microfiche and CD-ROM formats. Most large libraries and archives hold copies of at least one form of the IGI. You should regard all indexes and copies only as finding aids and wherever possible refer to the original entry or a filmed copy of the original to ascertain the formally recorded details which often include greater information.

5. Jews, Quakers, Nonconformists & Roman Catholics

Non-Anglican Marriage

Prior to the Reformation in the British Isles the established Christian faith was Roman Catholic. Some Jews had been brought to England from Rouen in 1066 by William the Conqueror, but in 1290 all Jews had been expelled "for ever" by Edward I. This was reinforced by making the inter-marriage in England of Jew and Christian a felony [5.1]. Matrimonial matters had been identified as the Church's responsibility by the Crown, as explained in preceding chapters, and so all valid marriages celebrated by a priest would have been within the Roman Catholic faith. Most of these ceremonialized marriages were unrecorded, as indicated above, as were other types of valid marriage at this time, for example the mutual exchange of promises.

From the Reformation, apart from a brief period during the reign of Queen Mary I, the Established Church in England has been Anglican and Protestant. Initially all those enjoying dissenting faiths, Jews and Christians not conforming to the Established Protestant Church, were banned from conducting, even attending, services including the solemnization of matrimony. Hence valid marriages for all dissenters were either not registered, or they were recorded in the registers of the Anglican, normally parish, churches, following a nuptial blessing or marriage service. Among the dissenting Christians were Quakers, Roman Catholics and many other Protestants who, with immigrant groups as well, became known collectively as Nonconformists.

Gradually, as the 17ᵗʰ Century progressed, religious toleration gained momentum and dissenting congregations began to meet, initially under utmost secrecy, then behind shutters, then quite openly. Some congregations kept meticulous records of their services and practices while others initially kept no records at all, for fear of the documents being used as evidence to declare their meetings illegal once more. Under Oliver Cromwell, Jews were permitted to settle in England for the first time in over 400 years. Protestants, such as Huguenots, immigrated into England fleeing from harsh Catholic persecution in Continental Europe. In general, marriage within all faiths in the British Isles followed remarkably similar patterns to those of the Established Church. The dissenting groups felt they were outside canon law, but when it came to marriage, they were compelled to recognize its influence as the civil authorities passed marital questions to ecclesiastical lawyers. These groups were also compelled to observe all temporal statutes, including the relatively few regarding marriage, degrees of impediment, the Puritan requirement for a magistrate to celebrate the marriage, and so on, as outlined in Chapter 2.

Prior to 1645, if any non-Anglicans celebrated marriage in their own way, and the parties were legally free to marry, such marriages may well have been valid, even if irregular. As with Anglicans, the difficulty was having evidence that the marriage, specifically the exchange of vows, had taken place. From 1660 to 1753, the situation was the same. Hardwicke's Act, and the 1823 Act, forbade marriages in unlicensed buildings, and as most non-Anglican places of worship were not licensed, this Act forced many non-Anglican marriages into the Anglican parish churches and registers.

However, Jews and Quakers had been keeping extremely lucid and precise records of their marriages and other religious events. Thus when Lord Hardwicke required better administrative arrangements for marriages, publishing banns, issuing licences, keeping registers and so on, Jews and Quakers (but no other dissenters) were specifically exempt from the Act. From 1754 much of the secular matrimonial legislation specifically mentions Jews and Quakers to be included or exempt. During the 19th Century there were many Parliamentary Acts concerned with marriages solely between couples of the Jewish or the Quaker persuasion such as the Quakers & Jews Marriages Validation Act 1847 [5.2], or the Marriage (Society of Friends) Act 1860 [5.3] and the Marriage (Society of Friends) Act 1872 [5.4].

As described in Chapter 2, the 1836 Registration Acts required marriages by all non-Anglican denominations to be notified to the Superintendent Registrar of the District where the marriage was planned, or where one party lived. In the case of Jews and Quakers, such details were taken care of by a Synagogue Secretary or a Friends' Registering Officer.

Marriage and other registers kept by non-Anglicans in England and Wales were reviewed in the 19th Century at the same time as Anglican non-parochial registers. Hence in 1840 [5.5] and again in 1858 [5.6] many of these were deposited with the Registrar General in London. These are now in the Public Record Office in the RG4 and RG6 (pre-1840) and RG8 (up to 1858) series. Most Roman Catholic congregations, apart from 79 mostly in Yorkshire, declined to surrender their registers. County record offices usually have microfilm copies of non-parochial registers relating to their counties.

The marriage rites and ceremonies of Anglicans are described in Chapter 4, but some information on those of Jews, Quakers, Nonconformists in general, and Roman Catholics is provided here.

Jews

In 1656 Oliver Cromwell invited a Jewish community to return to the British Isles, leasing out some land in London for a synagogue and a burial ground. The Sephardi Jews from Portugal and Spain, who came to England in 1656, and the Ashkenasi Jews from Germany and Poland in 1690, conducted their marriage ceremonies in their synagogues or in private houses; but in all cases they kept careful records of their marriage contracts (*ketubahs*) and marriage registers, see below.

Within a Jewish community marriage to one's deceased brother's widow was encouraged if she or her children were otherwise to become destitute. But this was strictly forbidden under canon and civil law in the British Isles until 1921 (see Chapter 2). To comply with both requirements, several marriages of British Jews were celebrated in continental Europe, although there may be references to these marriages in Jewish archives, and even newspapers, in the British Isles.

To be recognized as a Jewish marriage, both parties must be practising Jews. Details of the proposed marriage are collated by the bridegroom's Synagogue Secretary for formal registration. The marriage may be conducted in a synagogue or private house and at any time (unlike most other marriages in England and Wales) on any day except Saturday - the Jewish Sabbath. In the British Isles today there are several denominations of the Jewish faith gathered under particular synagogues. In London is the United Synagogue, in the central tradition, the right-wing Federation of Synagogues, and the Union of Orthodox Hebrew Congregations even further to the right. Outside London, across the remainder of the British Isles, are the left-wing Liberal and Reform Synagogues. The marriage ceremonies of each denomination are somewhat different.

When marrying at a United Synagogue the bride and groom, having fasted all that day to acknowledge repentance, stand with both sets of parents under a 'chuppah', a canopy or care-cloth, signifying the tents in which the Israelites originally lived. Other relations and guests sit behind, of whom at least ten must be male (who all wear hats) and two others are witnesses unrelated to the bridegroom or bride; the latter are formally approved by the bridegroom at the commencement of the service. The bride wears pure white, a veil and no jewellery to illustrate equality in wealth and life. The couple is given a homily of spiritual and practical advice by the rabbi celebrating the marriage. Originally this was the betrothal part of the ceremony which took place up to a year before the marriage proper. These days, the two ceremonies are truncated and run together. The groom takes the plain wedding ring and says to his bride "Behold, thou art consecrated unto me by this ring, according to the Law of Moses and of Israel". He then places the ring on the first finger of the bride's right hand (this finger symbolizes acquisition) and the Hebrew marriage contract is read, the bridegroom saying:

"Be thou my wife according to the Law of Moses and of Israel. I faithfully promise that I will be a true husband unto thee. I will honour and cherish thee; I will work for thee; I will protect and support thee; and will provide all that is necessary for thy due substance, even as it beseemeth a Jewish husband to do. I also take upon myself all such further obligations for thy maintenance during thy lifetime as are prescribed by our religious statutes". It is at this point that the marriage is deemed to commence.

The bride then promises to be true and faithful and to love, honour and cherish the groom. The Seven Benedictions are then recited in Hebrew and the marriage contract, also in Hebrew, is signed by the two witnesses. A marriage covenant in English is also signed, stating that the marriage has taken place according to the usage of Israel and the couple have exchanged their vows and plighted their troth to each other; a translation of the substance of the vows is printed on the ketubah, the signed contract.

The married couple then each drink wine twice from the same glass, demonstrating that they are about to share each other's lives, following which the husband smashes the glass, not to illustrate the frailty of marriage without love, as some books claim, but to express dismay and mourning at the loss of the Temple and to show that nothing can deter a Jew from promising to "set Jerusalem above my chiefest joy".

The rabbi pronounces the final blessing and a psalm is sung while the register is signed. The couple then spend a few moments alone (*yihud*) while they break their fast denoting their new status as a married couple. They then join their family and guests for the wedding banquet.

Registers of ketubahs are held at Synagogues, names and addresses of which may be found in the *Jewish Year Book*. Registers of some United Group synagogues are at their headquarters [5.7] in London. Registers of defunct congregations are likely to be in the Anglo-Jewish Archives at the Mocatta Library [5.8]. Some Jewish marriage registers have been published and others are included in literature of the Jewish Historical Society of England [5.9].

Quakers

Quakers, or members of the Religious Society of Friends, grew out of the preaching of George Fox in the north of England in 1647. They were nicknamed Quakers in 1650 by a magistrate when their teaching was declared blasphemous. Their administrative structure was set up in 1666 but records of meetings began in 1654. A religious meeting of a local congregation was (and is) termed a Particular Meeting, conducting its business from the 18th Century at a Preparative Meeting. Representatives from a Preparative Meeting attended a district Monthly Meeting and the Monthly Meetings, originally from within a county, send representatives to a Quarterly Meeting. Representatives from the latter attend the annual Yearly Meeting every Spring, the first of which was in London in 1668.

Hardwicke's requirements for marriages to be celebrated from 1754 only after the issue of a marriage licence or the reading of banns and in buildings licensed for publishing banns, did not apply to Quakers (or Jews). However, from the 1836 Act the local civil Superintendent Registrar had to be notified of every marriage, though the Friends' Registering Officer took care of that.

Before a Quaker marriage can take place permission has to be obtained from the Monthly Meeting to ensure there are no impediments - the bride and groom should both be free to marry and both sets of parents should give their consent. If either party comes from another county, or from a Particular Meeting under the jurisdiction of a different Monthly Meeting, that party has to provide the written clearance (by means of a certificate) of that Meeting that there is no impediment to the marriage. The Society these days has its own Registering Officer for each Monthly or Quarterly Meeting to ensure that their own religious, and the civil, requirements are being met.

The ceremony itself involves the couple or the groom alone making a declaration at an open meeting. Usually the bride and groom sit quietly surrounded by guests and relations; when they feel inspired the couple stand and hold hands, saying:

"Friends, I take this, my Friend Mary Jones, to be my wife, promising through Divine assistance, to be unto her a loving and faithful husband, as long as we both on Earth shall live".

At this point the two become married and sign the marriage certificate. The declaration and signing are observed by two relations or guests who also sign the certificate to demonstrate they have witnessed the ceremony and signatures of the bride and groom; after the meeting the whole congregation is invited to sign the certificate, so providing you with a treasure chest of names with which to appease your historical appetite. No rings are required although in some cases they are given or exchanged after the declaration. Permission from a Monthly Meeting was not always forthcoming, in which case the couple "married out", undergoing an Anglican ceremony at the local parish church.

In their marriage and other registers, Quakers often did not use names for days of the week or for months of the year; some of their records reflect this. Sunday was the First Day. Prior to 1752, March was the First Month; from 1752, January has been the First Month. Registers of marriage were kept by each Particular Meeting and permission to marry was given by the Monthly Meetings and collected together by the Quarterly Meetings.

Before their registers were deposited at the Public Record Office (PRO) in the 19th Century (see above) the Quakers made two sets of abstracts or "Digest" copies of them all. One set is now held centrally at the Friends' House in London [5.10], arranged by Quarterly Meetings, and each Meeting holds its own second set. The originals are in the RG6 and RG8 series at the PRO. Whilst the Digests are beautifully written and a delight to use, they do not contain witnesses' names; if you want to see these you must consult the originals or microfilm copies. Many Quaker records, including marriage registers after 1857 have been deposited in the local county record offices, some are at Friends' House, others are retained by the Meetings. The addresses of the local Registering Officers or Custodians of the records can be found in the annual *Book of Meetings* [5.11].

Nonconformists in General

The procedures of the marriage ceremonies of most Nonconformists, such as Congregationalists, Baptists and Methodists, are derived from those of the Anglican Church. Usually there is less ornamentation in the dress of the celebrant and of many couples and their attendants. The service is often succinct but equally sincere, with the recital of the vows being almost identical.

There is a comprehensive list of Nonconformist groups, and the dates when they became established in the British Isles from 1571 to 1879, in the Cameo *Tracing Your British Ancestors* [5.12]. Some of these communities originated within the Anglican Church and their marriages are recorded in parish registers. Whilst other Nonconformist congregations did not celebrate marriages at their own places of worship, their church records may indicate marriages of their members and where the event took place, such as the local parish church or a far away Nonconformist church or chapel. For centuries Dissenters have been prepared to travel long distances to worship according to their particular beliefs.

Some of the Nonconformist congregations that did maintain their own marriage registers in the 19th Century surrendered them in 1840 and 1858 and they are now in the Public Record Office in the RG4 and RG8 series. Others have subsequently been deposited in county record offices or in libraries of denominational historical societies [5.13]. Most County Record Offices (CROs) have microform copies of the Nonconformist registers in their areas and some registers have been transcribed and indexed. CRO staffs can advise what is available for their areas.

Roman Catholic Marriages

Because of the historic suspicion of "papists and popish people", which has been reviewed extensively above, Roman Catholics were the last of the non-Anglican faiths to be permitted to conduct marriages with the minimum of intervention from the "establishment". The 1791 Catholic Relief Act [5.14] permitted Roman Catholics to worship in their own churches provided the buildings and the clergy were registered. This proved of great benefit to those fleeing from the French Revolution. Many more Roman Catholic churches and chapels were built after the 1829 Emancipation Act [5.15], enabling Catholics to vote, to sit in Parliament, and to hold property unconditionally. Nonetheless, there are many early 19th Century marriages which are recorded in both Roman Catholic and Anglican registers. After the 1836 Marriage and Registration Acts (see Chapter 2) , civil registration gave Catholics (and everyone else in England) an opportunity to undergo a civil ceremony, which many preferred to a religious service following Anglican rites.

A marriage at a Roman Catholic church between two Catholics is celebrated during the service of Mass, on which occasion it is termed a Nuptial Mass. If only one party is Catholic, usually the Communion is omitted and hence the service takes place "outside of Mass".

The celebrant meets the couple at the church door and leads them to the altar, and then the service takes an almost identical form to that of the Anglican Church, although the ring or rings are more significant. After the priest has said to the couple "I join you together in marriage, in the name of the Father and of the Son and of the Holy Ghost, Amen", he sprinkles them with holy water. The bridegroom places the ring on the book, with pieces of gold and silver which the priest blesses. The bridegroom then gives the gold and silver to the bride saying "With this ring, I thee wed: this gold and silver I give thee; with my body I thee worship; and with all my worldly goods I thee endow". He then places the ring successively on the thumb, the index finger, the second and third fingers, saying "In the name of the Father, and of the Son, and of the Holy Ghost, Amen".

Concluding prayers include "Let the yoke of love and of peace be upon her. Let her be lovely in the eyes of her husband, even as was Rachel; let her be wise, as was Rebekah; let her live long and be faithful, as was Sarah. Let the author of mischief have no part in any of her doings".

Marriage registers of many Catholic Churches and chapels are held by the priests or the Catholic Diocesan authorities. Addresses are given in the *Catholic Directory*. In some cases the Catholic authorities have deposited the registers in the local county record offices. The Catholic Record Society [5.16] has published many registers and a half-yearly journal, *Recusant History*, with some references to Roman Catholic marriage. There is at least one index, specifically to some 30,000 Catholic marriages (c.1750-1870) in the London area, held by the Institute of Heraldic & Genealogical Studies [5.17]. There is a Catholic Family History Society [5.18].

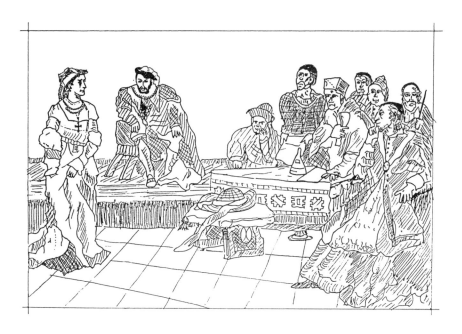

Based on "The First Trial of Queen Katherine" by Henry Gillard Glindoni (1852- 1912). The annulment of the marriage between Katherine of Aragon and Henry VIII was a milestone in matrimonial history, as explained in Chapter 2.

6. Settlements, Sales & Covenants

From time immemorial it had been traditional after a betrothal for a bride to be handed to the bridegroom in consideration of "coemption" (money paid down) - a sale-marriage as opposed to a rape-marriage or marriage-by-capture (both of which are described in Chapter 3). Early English laws [6.1] frequently refer to buying women and wives. This deal was considered to be quite respectable and totally different to the sale of a chattel or even a slave girl, there being an element of buying and selling in the marriage arrangements as both purchaser and vendor were intimately involved.

There were four reasons for the respectability: firstly the bride's father was paid a sum (the bride-price) as compensation for the loss of a useful worker; secondly the marriage contract involved the bride's father paying (in the form of a dowry - really the bridegroom-price, though never termed such) the bridegroom to protect his daughter and to secure for her a worthy position as the groom's companion and team-mate; thirdly the bride was not merely swapped for cash as she did not sever links with her kinsfolk who continued to pay for her misdeeds; fourthly the bridegroom, in effect, held the money in trust during his lifetime and made contractual arrangements for her to be provided for after his death. You may recall from the Biblical account in the Book of Genesis [6.2] that Jacob had no bride-price with which to buy Rachel and so had to serve her for seven years. On the other hand it is clear from the biography of Abraham, also related in Genesis [6.3], that the Canaanites practised marriage-by-capture. Today's symbolisms of the buying/selling element are described in Chapter 8.

By Anglo-Saxon times no man could lawfully marry without prior permission of the woman's *mundbora* (guardian) who was her father if still living. If consent was not forthcoming and they proceeded with the marriage, the husband was liable to penalties and he had no legal rights over his wife or her goods. In case of agreement, the man paid a *mede* (a present) for the privilege to marry the woman. On the morning after their wedding, the bridegroom gave his bride a *mogengabe* (morning gift) for her separate use (pin or pocket money).

Marriage settlements grew out of the mediaeval contracts and a reasonably consistent form was gradually established. The bride's father paid a dowry (tocher in Scotland) in cash and the bride-groom made the settlement on himself, then on his wife and then on any children of that marriage. Some documents arising from these settlements have survived. Within the settlement is often a detailed description of the property (the land settled) of both spouses and which issue (children and dependants) would benefit from what property. Sometimes the settlement was drawn up after the marriage, but the documentation makes this clear.

Marriage settlements in England, Wales and Scotland were personal documents and so, only by chance, are likely to have found their way into county or similar record offices. Many have been sold on junk stalls for fabrication into lamp shades, although a few have been rescued by discerning historians and then directed to record offices, museums or collections such as those of the Society of Genealogists [6.4]. Some Scottish marriage settlements and contracts have been preserved among the Registers of Deeds or a Register of Sasines in the Scottish Record Office. In contrast, Irish marriage settlements were registered and deposited with the Register of Deeds from 1708 (see Chapter 7). Marriage settlements and contracts in the Channel Islands survive among some family papers; those for the Isle of Man, and well documented [6.5], are held in Manx Museum Library, with archives relating to deeds' registration and probate.

Marriage settlements were specifically identified in some 19th Century legislation. An Act in 1833 [6.6], attempted to abolish "fines and recoveries in England and substitute more simple modes of Assurance", but a further Act in 1857 [6.7] was needed to clarify how married women could dispose of reversionary interests in personal estate; in the latter Act any personal estate settled on a woman from a marriage settlement was excluded.

During the 18th Century the financial fortunes of brides of gentry were publicized through the columns of national and local newspapers; accordingly, details are available to us today in libraries [6.8], although as the 19th Century progressed this practice was phased out. For the impoverished, the lack of cash to submit as a dowry could debar a father from offering his daughter in marriage; in some parishes the community provided for such cases from doles collected at funeral wakes.

Allied to the buying and selling of brides was the manorial feature of buying and selling the wardship of minors. Indeed, in 1193 William Longchamp, Bishop of Ely, paid 220 Marks (see the Chapmans Records Cameo on Weights, Money and other Measures [6.9]) to Richard I for the wardship of Stephen Beauchamp and the right to marry him to whomsoever he pleased; such sales appear not uncommon around this time, although selling marriages of women was more popular. In Scotland a very similar system pertained. For more details on the influence of the manorial system on marriage see Chapter 8.

The sale of wives in the British Isles, quite distinct from buying or selling a bride, whilst illegal was not uncommon [6.10] in the 18th, 19th and even into the 20th Centuries. This practice is described in Chapter 9 as one (yet invalid) route to divorce.

Dower or endowment (terce in Scotland), arranged at the church door or porch, was intended to provide tangible and financial support for a wife and children, particularly in the event of her husband's death. The arrangements normally gave a widow a life interest in a minimum of a third of the freehold estate of the deceased, but she could be endowed with a greater amount, provided it was agreed at the outset. The customs associated with dower are described in Chapter 8.

7. Marriage in Scotland & Ireland

Contrary to common acceptance, marriage in Scotland and marriage in Ireland were remarkably similar to that in England and Wales. Indeed Scots marriages were almost identical to those of the English until brief changes in England from 1645 to 1660 and more permanent alterations in England after 1753 (Hardwicke's Act did not apply in Scotland or Ireland). Irish marriages were hardly affected by distant Rome until the 19th Century; even in 16th Century Ireland, polygamous marriage was still practised in some sections of Gaelic society [7.1]. Do not forget that the United Kingdom of Great Britain and Ireland, created in 1801, lasted only until 1922 when the Irish Free State, later Eire and then the Republic of Ireland, emerged from the southern counties of Ireland, governed from Dublin and responsible for its own marriage (and other) laws. The six northern counties of Ireland in the new United Kingdom of Great Britain and Northern Ireland generally kept marriage law determined by the Westminster Parliament, whilst the Republic of Ireland had quite different legislation, as outlined later in this chapter.

Scotland

Fortunately for our understanding of early Scottish attitudes to marriage, some lectures of 1530 (by William Hay, Vice-Principal of King's College Aberdeen) have survived on pre-Reformation canon law in Scotland [7.2]. But canonical guidance on matrimony was brushed aside from 1559 by the reformers. Under the influence of John Knox and his followers, the Scottish Parliament in 1560 banished Roman Catholicism and a *Book of Common Order* was introduced; matrimonial legislation was altered and handled in the Commissary Court of Edinburgh from 1563 by Commissaries appointed from the Faculty of Advocates. The impediments of consanguinity and affinity were reduced and spiritual affinity was abolished. Divorce for adultery was introduced (a marked difference to English law - see Chapter 9). However, the sole requirement for a valid marriage - mutual consent - remained; the presence of a priest was not needed in Scotland for a valid marriage (but was needed from 1641 [7.3] for a legal marriage - see below). Scots delighted as much as Protestant English in spurning the Roman Catholic Council of Trent (Chapter 3). The Scottish parallel to the Anglican Church of England became the Episcopal Church of Scotland.

Scottish Episcopal Church marriage registers began in the 16th Century following Thomas Cromwell's exhortation in 1538, but with little enthusiasm, unlike English parish registers, even though encouraged by the General Provincial Council of Scotland. The Council required records of banns to be kept from 1552, but few places complied; in Scotland banns were proclaimed, rather than published, hence they were sometimes colloquially termed "proclamations". In 1616 the General Assembly required every minister to keep a register of marriages (and baptisms and burials), and this was confirmed by the Scottish Privy Council; but some places did not begin to maintain records until the late 18th Century.

From the Reformation, after some brief returns to episcopacy, the Church in Scotland became largely Presbyterian. In fact following the 1707 Union with England, an Act was needed in 1711 [7.4] to repeal the Scottish Act of 1695 [7.5] which had ejected Episcopalian clergymen and labelled the marriages and baptisms performed by them as irregular. From 1711 such ordained clergy in Scotland were able to legally conduct services, including those of matrimony. As a condition, the clergy had to swear an Oath of Allegiance to the Crown (Queen Anne) and renounce the Pretender. The Sheriffs were to ensure that Episcopalian services were not disturbed; any abusers were fined £100.

Meanwhile, the Crowns of England and Scotland had been linked through the Scottish James VI being crowned James I of England. As in England, anti-Catholicism grew into anti-Establishmentism, but vandalism to Catholic works of art and records was far more pronounced in Scotland than in England with the result that most Scottish church records, if kept, including any of marriage, were destroyed. In 1643 the Solemn League and Covenant, agreed between the Scots and the English Parliamentarians, expressed Scottish support for Puritan policies to counteract Irish championing of Charles I. The Scottish Parliament published a table of forbidden kinship in 1649 (see Appendix II), and declared that anyone marrying a forbidden relative was guilty of incest for which the punishment was death.

An Act of 25 July 1834 [7.6], referring to the 1661 and 1698 Acts [7.7] of the Scottish Parliament, repealed those sections which forbade Roman Catholic Priests, and other ministers not belonging to the Established (Presbyterian) Church of Scotland, from conducting marriages. And so with marked Catholic immigration from Ireland, and with the 1843 Disruption (split) in the Church of Scotland, many families seeking solace ventured into Nonconformity and Catholicism; some remained in the Established Church, others formed the Free Church of Scotland. Many registers of these congregations may be found in the Scottish Record Office (SRO) [7.8] although some are still with their ministers. Marriages, in general, are poorly recorded and few copies of registers have been published.

The Old Parish Registers (pre-1855 books, commonly called Old Parochial Registers) of the thousand or so Scottish parishes were called in by the Registrar General during 1855, at the start of Scottish civil registration - but not the start of civil marriage (see below); they are now mostly at New Register House, Edinburgh [7.9]. The registers have all been microfilmed; a few have been published. Some marriage registers record only the proclamation of banns, not the subsequent marriage which, of course, may not have taken place, or may have been celebrated elsewhere. The names of "cautioners" for both the groom and bride are occasionally included in banns registers; these persons ensured that their party did not back out of the planned marriage.

Marriages were sometimes alternatively, or also, recorded in Kirk Session minutes, many of which are in the SRO, although some are retained locally. The Kirk Session account books often show the fees paid on proclamation of the banns. As on an English manor (see Chapter 2), some Highland landlords maintained the right to permit the marriage of a tenant. Some of these records into the mid-19th Century have survived, to a much later date than in England.

Copious theses have been written about Scottish marriage, indicating how different it was in form from elsewhere; but this can only be because those authorities have not studied English marriage before the 18th Century. Or perhaps they have accepted, quite erroneously in common with most English observers, including the misfounded judgements of the House of Lords in 1844 and 1861 [7.10], that English marriages were always conducted in the presence of an episcopally ordained clergyman. Hopefully readers of this Cameo, based on the previous chapters, appreciate that in England or Wales a valid marriage originally required neither celebrant nor witness, only mutual agreement between man and woman without lawful impediment, to become husband and wife.

The contrast is largely that the Scots for years have widely [7.11] discussed these and termed them irregular marriages, which continued mostly unchanged until 1939, whereas the English have rarely exposed theirs (particularly those before the late-17th Century) which were severely restrained after 1753. The other important factor is that most exponents on Scottish marriage fail to point out that from 1641 until 1711 (and possibly until 1834) their irregular marriages may have been valid under canon law, but they were certainly illegal under secular law, ignored but not specifically repealed until 1834. Marriage Acts of the Scottish Parliament in 1641 and 1649 (and unlike much other legislation, re-enacted in 1661, 1695 and 1698) made it an offence for any marriage to be conducted except before a Church of Scotland minister. Hence clandestine and nonconformist marriages were outlawed. These Acts may have been ignored then, as well as by historians since, but they were legally binding until the Act of 1711, perhaps until the 1834 Scottish Marriage Act.

From earliest times, three types of valid marriage in Scotland were identical [7.12] to those in England: following the notification of intention to marry; an espousal of present words, "I do", at which the marriage commenced - physical consummation was not required for validity; and an espousal of future words, "I will", followed by sexual intercourse, at which the marriage was deemed to have commenced. (Note: normally no ecclesiastical licence could precede marriage, as in England or Ireland - although very occasionally a similar licence was granted by Church officials from 1638 [7.13].) The first type of valid marriage was, and is today, termed regular marriage both north and south of the Border. In Scotland the latter two types, although irregular, continued to be available as valid marriages (provided the espousal agreement and the intercourse had taken place in Scotland), until the 1939 Marriage (Scotland) Act [7.14], effective from 1 July 1940. However, neither of these irregular marriages was valid in England from 1645 to 1660, nor from 1753 to 1822, nor after 1836. In England from 1660 to 1753 such marriages tended to be termed clandestine as there were normally no witnesses; but without a celebrant or any religious or secular ceremony they were, naturally, also irregular. Because of the restraints and financial impositions on marriage ceremonies and registration, very many couples, particularly from northern English counties in the 18th and early 19th Centuries, popped into Scotland for marriage. As a consequence a 21-day residential qualification in Scotland was introduced from 1 January 1857 by Lord Brougham's 1856 Marriage (Scotland) Act [7.15], attempting to curb the attraction of midnight-flit elopement by couples from England.

In Scotland a fourth type of valid (but also irregular) marriage, by cohabitation with habit and repute, was possible following an Act of 1503 and is still legally available today, confirmed by the 1939, 1977 and 1980 Marriage and Reform Acts [7.16] (it was, however, also an offence under the 1641 and later Marriage Acts of the Scottish Parliament). In this case there is a tacit agreement to marry, implied by, and combined with uniform and undivided cohabitation in Scotland as husband and wife, with no legal impediments. The cohabitation cannot be as man and mistress or man and housekeeper, and must be sufficiently long, normally about a year, for the court to infer that the couple tacitly agreed to marry. If a substantial number of friends and relatives know the pair are not married and are merely contemplating marriage or cohabiting without intending matrimony, the doctrine of this type of irregular marriage does not apply. The present legal procedure is for one party to raise an action in the Court of Session for a declarator of marriage. If the Court is convinced there has been a tacit consent, and sufficient time has elapsed for cohabitation with habit and repute, a declarator may be granted. The Principal Clerk of Session then passes details to the Scottish Registrar General who registers the marriage according to Section 21 of the 1977 Act. This type of marriage is hardly used nowadays, there are about two per year, and most Scots undergo regular marriages.

The General Register Office and Registrar General in Scotland came into being on 1 January 1855 following the 1854 Act [7.17], but it proved too unwieldy as the clerks could not handle the details asked for, particularly when registering a birth. Some modifications were soon made on 15 June 1855 [7.18]. The principles for civil marriage registration were the same as for England and Wales and Ireland; however, until 1939 there was no concept of a civil ceremony by a Superintendent Registrar. The schedules to even the modified Acts clearly indicated that more particulars than on an English, Welsh or Irish couple were to be provided and recorded in registers and on certificates: eg, for both parties, full name, rank or profession, marital status, age, residence, father's name and profession and mother's name and maiden name. A further Act in 1860 [7.19] set up a Register of Neglected Entries to enable any marriages (and births and deaths) which had taken place in Scotland between 1800 and 1855 and not been recorded in the Old Parish Registers, to be formally registered for five shillings. Also by this Act certain sections of the 1854 and 1855 Acts were repealed, errors in registers prior to 1855 could be corrected and the pre-1820 Parish Registers were to be transmitted, under the Sheriff's direction, to the Registrar General in Edinburgh. Marriages and other events of Scottish subjects taking place out of Scotland since 1854 could be recorded in The Foreign Register held at the Scottish General Register Office.

An Act of 1878 "to encourage Regular Marriages in Scotland" [7.20] from 1 January 1879, enabled all clergymen, Quakers and Jews to celebrate marriages after publication of the intention to marry; a Registrar's Certificate was to have the same validity as publishing banns before a regular marriage. 15 days residence in the registrar's district was required and a fee of 1s 6d was payable for the intention to be registered in the Marriage Notice Book., similar to the situation in England. After 7 days, if no objection was received, the Registrar could, for a shilling, issue a certificate to one of the couple to authorize a minister to conduct the marriage. Schedules to the Act identified formats for the Notice and the authorization. Non-compliance, false entries etc. were punishable.

The 1939 Marriage Act, which simplified irregular marriages, has been mentioned above but most provisions were radically changed and further simplifications introduced by the Marriage (Scotland) Act 1977, slightly modified in 1980 [7.21]. Two types of regular marriage, and one irregular (explained above), remain. The regular marriage, either a civil or a religious ceremony, must be preceded by giving notice to the Registrar of the District where the marriage is to be solemnized. There is no residential qualification. The party giving notice submits his or her birth certificate, marital status and address, the fee, names of both parties and proposed wedding date. This information, without addresses, is displayed in the Registration Office, normally for 14 days to allow for any objections. If there are none, the District Registrar issues a Marriage Schedule. For a civil marriage he retains this until the ceremony, normally conducted in his office in the presence of two witnesses over 16. For a religious ceremony the Schedule is taken by the couple to the minister, which gives him licence to celebrate the marriage; it is then signed by both parties, two witnesses over 16 and the minister, and returned within three days to the Registrar to enter the event in his register. Scottish civil and religious marriages can be conducted at any time, as arranged in advance and stated on the Schedule.

Records of the irregular marriages conducted at Gretna Green are held at Ewart Library, Dumfries; those conducted at Lamberton Toll, Berwickshire, held at the Scottish Record Office (SRO), have been published. A Scottish couple whose irregular marriage had been discovered may have been reprimanded by a Kirk Session and so recorded in its minutes. For details on other irregular marriages in Scotland see the Society of Genealogists (London) Leaflet No.10.

As mentioned above, divorce on the ground of adultery was recognized in Scotland from the Reformation. In 1573 [7.22], divorce for desertion also became possible. Cases until 1830 were heard in the Commissary Court of Edinburgh, thereafter the Court of Session was responsible;

records of both courts are in the SRO. Cases from 1658 to 1800 were catalogued and an index published by the Scottish Record Society in 1909. Cases of fornication, and disciplining the parents of any resulting illegitimate children, were usually dealt with by the Kirk Sessions and may be found in their minutes, also at the SRO. Adultery and desertion remained the only two grounds for divorce for nearly 400 years under Scottish law. In 1938 [7.23] cruelty, incurable insanity, sodomy and bestiality were added to possible grounds for divorce in Scotland, modified slightly in 1964 [7.24] and revised in the Divorce (Scotland) Act 1976 [7.25]. Unlike England, the subsequent marriage of the parents usually legitimated a bastard, although the Crown could also provide legitimation, at any age; those records are with the Privy Council documents in the SRO. A published, indexed, calendar of these records from 1484 to 1584 and from 1660 is available at the SRO. The records from 1585 to 1659 are not indexed.

Joan Fergusson's *Directory of Scottish Newspapers* (see Bibliography) is useful for identifying potential sources of reports of marriages in Scotland and of Scots elsewhere.

Ireland

In Ireland, as far back as 1172, at a Council of Cashel held under Henry II, it was decreed [7.26] "that all Christians in Ireland, repudiating their incestuous connexions with their kindred and relations, [should] contract lawful marriages". The curious Statute of Kilkenny (1367), establishing the English Pale in and around Dublin, decreed that anyone of English origin marrying into an Irish family was guilty of high treason. This was hardly compatible with Pope Adrian IV having granted Ireland to King Henry II (1155-89) and the English sovereigns thereafter being termed Lords in Ireland. Henry VIII tidied up the situation in 1542 [7.27]. An added problem was the split in the Church in Ireland between those who favoured hereditary succession of the parochial clergy (and hence supported marriage of priests) and those who advocated celibacy (and so were unable to support hereditary succession). Obviously the former welcomed the Protestant Reformation, enabling clergy to marry; but a common view that the former were linked exclusively to erenhagh families and the latter influenced solely by coarbs, is challenged by Katherine Simms [7.28].

Clerical marriage was one issue but polygamy was also rife and an Act in 1634 enforcing monogamy was passed in the Irish Parliament only after considerable opposition from Catholics and Protestants in the Lower House; and in 1640 the Lords attempted to repeal this. Of course, we have seen that in England and Scotland valid marriage demanded no more than a couple agreeing to become husband and wife; it would seem the situation was identical in Ireland. In fact Sir John Popham, a late 16th Century Irish Attorney General, remarked that only one in twenty Irish marriages was celebrated in a church. Several commentators claim that the marriage ceremony was performed by a priest; and whilst most Catholics followed the 1563 Council of

Trent decision that canon law required the presence of a priest and two witnesses, a civil valid marriage needed neither. Further, as there had been no strong Puritan influence in Ireland, the Restoration did not create the same backlash into matrimonial laxity as in England. Yet the Catholic priests in the 16th and 17th Centuries [7.29] appear to have issued more than a few divorces on behalf of the Pope.

The Church of Ireland, Anglican and Episcopalian in form, was created by Henry VIII in 1537 [7.30] as the Established Church, formally breaking with Rome but retaining the existing [7.31] administrative structure of the Catholic Church, as had occurred in 1534 in England. However, Henry (or his advisers) failed to appreciate that most of the Irish, especially in rural areas, were not overzealous over any faith and spoke little English. Old Celtic (Brehon) law and traditions were deep-rooted in Ireland. In England, by translating marriage and other services and the Prayer Book and Bible into English, the authorities were able to promote the Reformed Protestant Church; hence all subsequent matrimonial (and other) matters were understandable, even if not agreeable, throughout England. But in Ireland no one dreamed of providing similar promotional literature in Irish for very many years [7.32] and few but the English immigrants were attracted (or persuaded) into the Reformed Church of Ireland. The Act of Union in 1801, which closed the Irish Parliament, gave the Church of Ireland the same particular rights and privileges in Ireland as the Church of England had in England, so much so that the Anglican Church in Ireland was officially termed the United Church of England and Ireland; these privileges were lost when the Irish Church was dis-established in 1869.

From 1634 clergy in the Established Church of Ireland were required to keep marriage (and baptism and burial) registers. Not many complied, particularly in rural areas in the south, although at least one starts in 1619. Parochial Returns, copies of the register entries, were also made by some clergy in the 19th Century. It should not be forgotten that Hardwicke's Act did not apply in Ireland. The 1727 Test Act, until repealed in 1778, required persons who wished to hold any office, own land or vote, to regularly attend Church of Ireland services. In addition, marriages of all denominations (unless licensed), and mixed marriages until 1845, had to be celebrated within the Established Church (of Ireland); others were void, identically to the situation in England. Hence when seeking a marriage of an ancestor of any denomination in Ireland at this period it is best to look first at the Church of Ireland registers.

Marriage in Ireland, as in England, followed banns or the grant of a Consistory (Common) Licence by a bishop or a, more expensive, Prerogative (Special) Licence by the Archbishop of Armagh from his Dublin seat (as did the Archbishop of Canterbury from his London seat). In Ireland, however, before about 1870 marriage by banns was practised by only the humblest in the community. Hence Irish marriage licence records (allegations, bonds etc.), are fruitful sources of information. Such material (1727-1845) for the Diocese of Armagh, covering much of the present Northern Ireland and County Louth, is now in the Public Record Office of Northern Ireland (PRONI) [7.33]. Records, if surviving, for the other dioceses of the Church of Ireland, such as indexes to Special Licences (1625-1857), are in the Irish National Archives in Dublin [7.34]. Extant banns records are with parish registers.

In 1875 and 1876 Parliamentary Acts [7.35] declared all pre-1870 Anglican marriage and other registers public documents, following the 1869 dis-establishment of the Church of Ireland, and required them to be deposited in the National Archives; about two-thirds of the parishes complied. In 1922 most of the originally deposited registers were destroyed. Fortunately many copies and extracts [7.36] had been made. Microfilm copies of the surviving material, including the Parochial Returns and the non-deposited registers are in the National Archives and, for the six northern counties, in PRONI. Original and surviving registers are today in a variety of places in Ireland, some in the National Archives, some in the Representative Church Body Library [7.37], some in PRONI, some with the incumbents.

However, contrary to many commentaries, Penal Laws in 1695 (repealed in 1829) were more favourable to Roman Catholics in Ireland than in England (where Catholicism was banned), perhaps tempered by the 1691 Treaty of Limerick. Accordingly, in Ireland, licensed Roman Catholic priests were able to conduct services and celebrate marriages according to the Council of Trent. From 1 May 1746 [7.38], until repealed by Acts in 1870 and 1871 [7.39], any marriage solemnized by a Roman Catholic priest was void if either party was, or ever had been, Protestant. (Until 1845 such mixed marriages were legal only when celebrated by an Anglican clergyman - see below.) Unfortunately there was no compulsion on the Catholic priests to keep marriage, or other, registers and whilst some Roman Catholic parish registers begin before 1695 (Wexford in 1671, Galway in 1690), most have few entries before 1830. Microfilm copies of 90% of the registers from the 26 Irish Catholic Dioceses are kept at the National Archives. PRONI has copies for the northern Roman Catholic dioceses.

In the early 17th Century, in an attempt to increase Protestant influence in Ireland, to ward off Catholic collusion with England's constant enemies Spain and France, James I "planted" Presbyterian families in Ulster from his native Scotland. Marriages of Irish Presbyterians were recorded in Kirk Session Minutes Books as well as in registers; the latter begin in 1674, although they become more prolific from 1819. Because of internal dissent, several branches of the Presbyterian Church emerged, each keeping its own registers. The 1678 Test Act applied not only to unlicensed Roman Catholics, but to all Nonconformists including Presbyterians. From 1839 to 1844 marriages between Presbyterians and Anglicans were legal only if celebrated in an Anglican Church. So Presbyterian marriages for these periods should be in Church of Ireland registers (see above). But several Presbyterian churches ignored the legislation; some of their marriage registers are now with the Presbyterian Historical Society [7.40].

Quakers were established in Ireland in 1654 and began keeping records in 1671. Copies of these, which include marriages, are at the Friends' offices in Dublin and Lisburn [7.41].

From 1747, Irish Methodists recorded their marriages and other vital events in Church of Ireland registers, but in 1816 Irish Wesleyan Methodists began to keep their own registers. Most of these, which include marriages, are still with the ministers.

Unlike the situation elsewhere in the British Isles, civil registration was introduced in Ireland in stages, following Parliamentary Acts in 1844 and 1863. These laid the foundations for a different approach to secular matrimonial law in Ireland, accentuated in 1922 at the creation of the Irish Free State, becoming Eire in 1937 and the Republic of Ireland in 1949. The framework had actually been set earlier in 1844 following the historically incorrect statement in the House of Lords (see Chapter 3) that for a marriage to be valid it had to be celebrated by an episcopally ordained clergyman. The 1844 Marriages (Ireland) Act [7.42] was based on that judgement; prior to then, as in England until 1837, marriage had been by mutual agreement (an espousal of present words) or by a promise to marry followed by intercourse (an espousal of future words plus consummation), or in church after the publishing of banns or granting of a licence. The civil registration of marriages of non-Catholics began on 1 April 1845 following the 1844 Act with its 85 sections and seven schedules. Slight amendments were made in 1845 [7.43] regarding parish unions, and in 1846 [7.44] if one party resided in England or Scotland, or the proposed venue for the marriage was not available. Other amendment Acts were passed in 1849 [7.45] also relating to church buildings, in 1860 [7.46] regarding Quakers, and in 1861 [7.47] regarding forged registers.

The 1863 Registration of Births and Deaths (Ireland) Act [7.48], in spite of its title, mentioned marriages, and the 1863 Marriage Law (Ireland) Amendment Act [7.49], amongst other changes, included Roman Catholic marriages; detailed arrangements were clarified later in 1863 in the Marriages Registration (Ireland) Act [7.50]. Hence full registration of all marriages, and births and deaths, in Ireland became effective on 1 January 1864. Even this required minor changes in 1870 [7.51] regarding stamp duties; in 1870 [7.52] and 1871 [7.53] as a result of the Dis-establishment Act; in 1872 [7.54] regarding Quakers again; and in 1873 [7.55] regarding marriages in places of worship not belonging to Roman Catholics or Protestant Christians.

Irish marriage certificates usually show similar information to that on English certificates, although until 1864 details on witnesses and fathers of the couple, though required, are often missing. Civil registration records and indexes for all of Ireland prior to 1922 and for the Irish Republic since 1922 are held by the Registrar General in Dublin [7.56]; those for Northern Ireland since 1922 are held by the Registrar General in Belfast [7.57]. PRONI has microfilm copies of birth, but not of marriage, indexes before 1922. Original registers of marriages in Northern Ireland are held in local District Registrars' Offices.

The legal age for marriage in the Republic of Ireland remained at 14 and 12 for boys and girls until 1 January 1975 [7.58], unlike 1929 in England, Wales and Scotland, when it was raised to 16, although application for marriage under 16 is possible to the High Court in Dublin. The age of majority, and hence the free age for marriage in Ireland, was reduced from 21 to 18 in 1985 [7.59]. Regarding prohibited degrees of kinship, the English Acts to 1922, including those of 1907 and 1921 applied, but not the 1931 Act (see Chapter 2).

Reports of Protestant and of Catholic weddings in Irish newspapers in the 18th and later centuries normally provide more details than entries in marriage registers or on civil certificates. PRONI has an excellent guide to newspapers relating to the six northern counties; the National Library [7.60] and Trinity College Library in Dublin [7.61] are good sources for newspapers in the Republic of Ireland.

Marriage settlements in Ireland were made either before or after the marriage, as in England (see Chapter 6). However, contrary to the English position, most Irish settlements were registered and papers may be found in the Registry of Deeds in Dublin [7.62], established in 1708.

Until 1746 Irish marriage licences were normally issued only if both parties were members of the Church of Ireland, although a few licences for Roman Catholics appear in the Protestant parish registers. From 1746 licences for mixed marriages were issued. The original bonds were destroyed in 1922 but fortunately abstracts were made from many of the licences by Sir William Betham and Gertrude Thrift. Indexes of the licences of Cloyne (by George T Green), of Cork and Ross (by Herbert W Gillman) and of Clonfert, Dublin, Killaloe, Ossary and Raphoe (by others) have been published [7.63].

Divorce in Ireland was originally handled as in England and Wales, namely by the Ecclesiastical Courts or through a Private Act of Parliament, as described in Chapter 9. However, the 1857 and 1884 Matrimonial Causes Acts in England did not apply in Ireland and the Church Courts' responsibilities for these matters continued in Ireland until 1870 when they passed to the High Court. Identically to the Church Courts, the High Court would grant only decrees of nullity, determining that a marriage had never come into being; a decree of dissolution, terminating a valid subsisting marriage, was not possible in the Republic of Ireland until November 1995. Article 41.3.2 of the 1937 Irish Constitution states "No law shall be enacted providing for the grant of a dissolution of marriage", thereby complying with canon law of the Roman Catholic Church. The 1922 Constitution of the Irish Free State contained no such prohibition but in three years only three petitions were presented. The 1937 position was confirmed by a public referendum on 26 June 1986 when 935,843 voted against amending the Constitution, 538,279 were in favour; the total electorate at that time was 2,440,907. Another referendum on 25 November 1995 produced a narrow majority in favour of civil divorce in the Republic of Ireland, providing couples had lived apart for four of the preceding five years.

8. British Courtship & Marriage Customs

Courtship Customs

Many couples in the British Isles today become engaged, indicating their intentions to marry, as in days gone by they would have been betrothed or espoused. An engagement nowadays is usually marked by the bride-to-be wearing a ring as a sign that she is affianced. Rings, being an unbroken circle of continuity, from the beginning of time have been worn as an outward sign of a permanent relationship. An Anglo-Saxon groom gave his bride a pledge at the betrothal and placed a ring on her right hand, it being transferred to her left hand at the nuptial blessing. Double espousal rings, gemels, were sometimes separated during an espousal ceremony, each party wearing one ring until the marriage proper. Some multiple rings had three parts, a witness wearing the third. Bracelets are sometimes worn instead of, or in addition to, rings, but all represent an unbroken circle of continuity or permanence. It has also been suggested that both bracelets and rings symbolize shackling, following the capture of the woman by the man in the former rape-marriage or marriage-by-capture discussed in Chapter 3. Rings have been made from various materials over the centuries; in ancient Ireland the man gave his potential mate a bracelet woven of his hair as a symbol of physical possession. A similar custom persisted in recent times with the girl carrying a lock of her fiancé's hair in a locket around her neck.

On their espousal, trothplight or engagement, many couples pick a ring because they admire the stone or it has an affordable design. Not infrequently the bride's birth stone is selected. Accepted birth stones and their customary meanings are:

January	garnet	constancy	July	ruby	love
February	amethyst	sincerity	August	sardonyx	married happiness
March	bloodstone	courage	September	sapphire	wisdom
April	diamond	innocence	October	opal	hope
May	emerald	success	November	topaz	fidelity
June	pearl	health	December	turquoise	harmony

Diamonds are often chosen from tradition, ancient alchemists believing that the sparkle of a diamond represented the fire of love, or perhaps the fire that keeps evil at bay. Other stones are used, set in a particular order for their initial letters to spell a significant message; for example, Lapis lazuli, Opal, Verde antique, Emerald: **LOVE**.

The gift of an engagement ring is presumed to be an absolute gift under the 1970 Law Reform Act [8.1], and so need not be returned if the engagement is broken. The presumption may, however, be rebutted if it can be proved that the ring was given on the condition, express or implied, that it should be returned if the marriage did not take place for any reason. Ailing and failed betrothals made up much of the business of Church Courts in the 16th and 17th Centuries.

"Bundling" or "tarrying" constituted a courtship custom, accepted by a poorer couple's parents, particularly in rural Wales into the 19th Century. A couple, fully dressed, shared the same bed on Saturday or Sunday nights, apparently to economize on heating and lighting [8.2]. Attempts in Dolgellau in 1840 failed to found a "Society to Suppress Bundling". The practice was encouraged also by poor families in Cambridgeshire. However, bundling does not appear to have been accepted as a contractual arrangement (in contrast to "hand-fasting" - see Chapter 3) and every case seems to have been followed by a formal marriage ceremony.

Courtship was formerly quite a communal affair, following the acceptance of a public betrothal. A boy and girl making their own choice of a partner became a peculiarly British custom, passed to her overseas colonies and dominions; but even then brothers and sisters or maids would accompany the couple as they went about their courting. This strange practice of self-choice was noted by many Continental European travellers and diarists visiting British shores.

Betrothal, in essence, placed courtship in the hands of a third party, usually the girl's father or older brothers (see Chapter 3). It was essential to make the right choice of a partner: "better be half-hanged than ill wed" [8.3]. Prior to 1858, once married there was no turning back; divorce was unattainable by the average couple (see Chapter 9). The arrangements in Ireland, at least into the 17th Century [8.4], were accompanied by copious draughts of strong whiskey from the "agreement-bottle". If after the wedding the bride died childless within an agreed time, the bridegroom's family was able to recover its side of the bargain, the bridegroom-price mentioned in Chapter 4. A betrothal party with similar drinking and terms was called a "booking" in Scotland, a "flouncing" in the Channel Islands. Arranged marriages are still common within some cultures, although many couples in the British Isles today prefer to believe there are feelings of mutual attraction, so leaning more towards the concept of espousal. Nevertheless, some modern couples, by using a computer dating agency or a lonely hearts' club as a match-making third party, merely reflect former betrothal procedures.

Forcible espousal, marriage-by-capture against the wishes of the maiden, termed "pretended marriage" in 1651 (see Chapter 2), was dealt with on the Isle of Man by a temporal customary law of 1577. "The deemster shall give her a rope, sword and a ring, and she shall have the choice to hang him with the rope, cut off his head with the sword, or marry him with the ring" [8.5]. Marriage-by-capture was still practised in Kilkenny County in 18th Century Ireland, according to a report concerning children of 12 and 14 in the *Gentleman's Magazine* of March 1767.

Some of the strictly Christian procedures of courtship and marriage gradually became symbolized over the years. The betrothal or espousal, the verbal contract and exchange of vows between spouses, was often marked by the exchange of love tokens. In Bedfordshire, Buckinghamshire and Northamptonshire, homes of pillow lace, wooden or bone lace bobbins, inscribed with the names of the spouses, were exchanged from the 16th to early 20th Centuries. Porcelain or china fairings were exchanged, particularly in the Midlands. Love spoons were carved from a single piece of wood and exchanged in Wales. Many couples broke a gold or silver coin in two at their espousal, each partner keeping half until the marriage when the parts, like the partners, were united.

The tradition of the bride-to-be collecting household items for her "bottom drawer" or "hope-chest" grew out of the dowry in the marriage-by-purchase arrangements; the dowry was passed to the bridegroom, not for his personal use as explained in Chapter 3, but for their mutual use, or even held in trust by him for her use after his demise. Many of the items, even in the 20th Century, were lovingly hand-stitched by the girl and embroidered with the initials of her beau and herself, though more recently they have been obtained from a catalogue store. The items that the bride collected for herself, her "trousseau" (little bundle), also have origins in the dowry.

In his *Bride of Abydos*, Lord Byron (1788-1824) suggested a future wife should be able:

> To soothe thy sickness, watch thy health,
> Partake but never waste thy wealth.
> Or stand with smiles unmurmuring by,
> And lighten half thy poverty.

"Marry your sons when you will, your daughters when you can".

"Honest men marry soon, wise men not at all".   [Old English proverbs]

Wedding-Day Customs

Almost all Christian wedding-day customs are derived from pagan fertility rituals and heathen rites, in which the whole community took part to engender happiness and to dismay, confuse or appease evil spirits. Numerous traditions and superstitions for which no credible origins could be ascertained, such as bridesmaids walking backwards three times round the church after the service to be sure of finding a sweetheart, are not included in this Cameo.

Hymen, the beautiful youth of Athens and god of marriage, was admired by all and hence "hymeneal gaiety" was a former term for wedding-day joy. Cupid, son of Venus and god of sensual love, is more popular today, particularly on wedding invitations and cards. Tilting at the quintain and dancing were always joyous. A wedding was a festive occasion, to be enjoyed by every parishioner, not just the families being linked through wedlock, and all looked forward to joining the revels. "Penny-weddings" (termed "siller marriages" in Aberdeenshire [8.6]) were organised for poorer couples unable to provide hospitality, at which everyone contributed their pennies for the community celebration. The Puritans strove to eliminate such "popish and heathen" behaviour; but succeeded only in separating the merry-making from the nuptial blessing, driving the former from the church to the green or into the pub where it has become our modern reception. Many of the old customs, some varied with modern materials, were still practised in the British Isles in the last century and some still survive today.

Pealing bells, banging gongs and blowing trumpets were originally intended to frighten away the devil. In Lincolnshire parishes, church tower bells were rung at the close of the service at which banns were read for the third time. The noise of "firing the anvil", by which the local blacksmith put a small charge of gunpowder in an indentation in his anvil and exploded it with a red-hot poker as the married couple passed his forge, also dispelled evil. Butchers' boys noisily beating on their cleavers supposedly similarly drove off evil spirits; until the mid-19th Century in many parts of the country these boys, wearing blue coats and white aprons, would stand outside a house where a wedding was taking place and play on their cleavers with knuckle bones. Some managed to "tang", to co-ordinate the clamour and produce recognizable sounds of "rough music", at a "shivaree". A more tuneful wedding song was called an "epithalamium" [8.7].

Besides noise, fire was expected to eradicate evil. Hence the burning of candles was incorporated into marriage (and other Christian) rites; women at their espousals were enjoined in 1256 [8.8] to come to the church with lighted candles. Hymen is always depicted bearing a burning torch. The bridal veil was originally of golden yellow, to simulate a flame (and termed a *flammeum*) and ward off evil spirits. White was introduced later as a sign of purity. However, the purpose of the veil itself was to signify submission and permanent obedience to the bridegroom, similar to nuns wearing veils to demonstrate their submission and permanent obedience to God. In the Bible,

Rebekah veiled herself on seeing Isaac [8.9]; many modern brides are probably unaware they are displaying any subservience to their husbands-to-be.

Evil spirits were kept out of the bride's home altogether by shutting all windows and doors tightly on her last night as a spinster, ending her "spinstering" (spinning) days, before she became a wife, progressing to "wifing" (weaving). In some parts of the country, chimneys were blocked up on the wedding day itself, which must have created a dilemma for those who wanted to light a fire to keep witches away.

The horseshoe, so often displayed at weddings, is an adaptation of the orb of the moon between cow's horns, the symbol of Isis, Egyptian goddess of procreation, Universal Mother of the living and protectress of the spirits of the dead. Isis, believed to prevent hysteria and lunacy, was so revered under various names by Greeks and Romans that a horseshoe was also fixed over the threshold to keep out the evil power of witches, and even the plague, and to keep luck within the home. Carried by a bride, or worn by women on their footwear, a horseshoe was believed to attract the good-will of Isis to attain success in love, happiness in motherhood, and fortune in life.

For very many years a bride has customarily worn:

> Something old, something new,
> Something borrowed, something blue.

Old to remind her of her old life with her family, new to look forward to a new life of married happiness, borrowed to symbolize help and support when needed from friends, and blue to symbolize loyalty. Some brides wore a knife or knives to indicate their involvement in kitchen activities: "See at my girdle hang my wedding knives", wrote Thomas Dekker in 1631 in *Match me in London*. A pair of decorated wedding knives, dated 1629, was exhibited at a meeting of the British Archaeological Association in 1860. Fire-tongs, keys and brooms were brandished by guests to similarly illustrate domesticity. The belief that a bride wearing only a chemise (or nothing at all) at her wedding absolved the bridegroom of all her debts for ever, appears to have waned by the 20th Century. This derived from the fact that until the late 19th Century a husband was responsible for his wife's debts "because on marriage he acquired an absolute interest in her personal estate; hence if he acquired no property with her [even clothing], he could not be compelled to satisfy the claims of her creditors" [8.10].

After the betrothal or espousal, when the couple had decided there was no turning back, it was traditional to cut the bride's hair to remove her beauty, making her unappealing to other suitors. Later modified so that her hair was cut immediately before the wedding; tradition has recently been modified yet again; she now goes to the hairdresser's on her wedding morning to appear particularly attractive to the guests. It has always been a relief for us all when the bride cries profusely on the wedding day as it demonstrates she is not a witch who, we are told, can shed only four tear-drops from her left eye.

The original reason for bridesmaids was to confuse the spirits as to the identity of the bride, and hence they dressed similarly to her. A chief bridesmaid, termed a "Matron-of-Honour" if herself married, was assisted by one, two or five others, nine or eleven in Victorian times; Royal weddings have traditionally had eight bridesmaids for several generations. A number of brides-maids around the bride also symbolize protecting her from attack by the groom in a marriage-by-capture.

In many parts of the country it was the custom for the marriage rite to be celebrated in the bride's home parish. In some large parishes there could be several chapelries a few miles apart to choose from; it was not uncommon for the one furthest from the bride's house to be chosen so giving the family an opportunity for a "day out". For the same reason a more distant parish was sometimes chosen, even though this may have resulted in an irregular or even a voidable marriage.

Formerly, a bride was collected from her home and led to the church by the bride's knights (the groom's men) while the bridesmaids led the groom to church. The following lines from a long poem by Edward Chicken (1698-1746) of Northumberland [8.11] illustrate this custom:

> Two lusty lads, well dressed and strong,
> Step out to lead the bride along:
> And two maids of equal size
> As soon the bridegroom's hands surprise.

Additionally to confuse the spirits it was customary for the best man, termed the groomsman until the 20th Century, not only to dress identically to the groom on the wedding day, but to sleep at the home of the bride on the night before; going out with only the groom and his friends, drinking to excess, is a recent practice. Royal weddings often had two supporters or groomsmen. These supporters, some now acting as ushers at the church, and even the solitary best man, are all that remain of the band who assisted in the marriage-by-capture of the bride.

The wedding guests wearing rosemary, frequently gilded or dipped in scented water, diverted the attentions of unwelcome spirits (similarly to garlic being employed to ward off vampires). Bay leaves were sometimes substituted for rosemary.

Presents from families and friends replaced the marriage settlements and financial contracts (see Chapter 6) between the bride's and bridegroom's families in the past. It is said that the giving of a ring replaced the sealing, with a signet ring, of the formal contract. Until the end of the 18th Century the giving of presents took place at a "purse and girdle" or a "bidding" - entertainments organized before the wedding. An account was preserved of who had given what and its value, in anticipation of the givers receiving presents of similar worth at their own weddings (a similar custom is practised today at Sikh weddings). In some districts, bidding invitations were printed and distributed, in other districts, notably Wales, the bidding was performed by a herald carrying a crook or wand adorned with ribbons. He rode in a decorated wain-cart in Cumberland.

At the nuptial ceremony in church, solidarity and support for a particular spouse was expressed by their families and friends standing or sitting immediately behind them. The couple stood at the chancel steps facing the altar with the bride on her groom's left, leaving his right (sword-bearing) hand free to defend them both throughout the rest of their lives (or resulting from the Genesis story that Eve was taken from a rib on Adam's left side). Thus the bride's adherents (the "spindle-side") occupied the north side of the church while the groom's followers (the "spear-side") were on the south. The couple originally stood under a canopy or "care-cloth" to shelter them from danger from above, a practice still observed at Jewish weddings (see Chapter 5).

The custom of the bride's father, or senior member of her family, giving her away during the ceremony is only a small step from the former practice of selling or exchanging her for the bride-price at the betrothal, described in Chapter 6. In past times it was more likely to have been a brother as many parents died before their children married. The purchase money or goods in kind, land, sheep, cattle or horses, etc, was termed a "wed", from which "wedding" derives.

Formerly at weddings the espousal ring was transferred to the bride's left hand, being placed successively on her thumb, second, third and fourth fingers, saying "in the name of the Father, Son and Holy Ghost, Amen". The fourth finger (counting the thumb as the first) of the left hand was chosen as it was believed to contain a vein leading direct to the heart. Virgins espoused to the Church wore the ring of their celestial nuptials on the right hand. During the reigns of George I and George II it was customary in England for a wedding ring to be worn on the thumb, as can be seen in portraits of the time - Lady Ann Clifford, Countess of Pembroke, for example. In Ireland widows in the Roman Catholic church wore a glove to distinguish them from virgins. In pre-Reformation times, and still practised today by some Roman Catholics (see Chapter 4), the wedding ring was blessed by sprinkling in the form of a cross with water; since the Reformation this has been replaced in the Established Church by laying the ring on the Prayer Book. In the 18th Century it was common to engrave the ring with a motto or poesy; today initials or names are inscribed. The separate parts of double rings, gemels, were often reunited on a bride's finger at the nuptial ceremony to signify uniting the bride and groom. Curtain rings or even a door key (noted in an Essex parish register in the early 19th Century) have been used in emergencies.

In 1855 [8.12], Parliament fixed the quality of gold wedding rings - a far cry from Pliny's time (AD 23-79) when wedding rings were of iron. Gold was probably not used for another hundred years, the time of Tertullian (160-230), since when it has been the traditional material. In the 13th Century it was decreed [8.13] that "the ring be not made of rushes or of other vile materials".

The bride and groom becoming one flesh was symbolized in a number of ways. For example, the couple joining hands, perhaps entwined by the priest's stole, during the marriage ceremony, and the proliferation of bows and knots; although the true-love knot has nothing to do with true or love but derives from the ancient Danish word *trulofa*, "I plight my troth" [8.14]. Invading Danes also introduced "favours" (enlaced ribbons, garlands of flowers, or corn in bows, top-knots and nosegays).

A sense of union was also shown by communal eating of cake and drinking of wine, originally in church, by all the witnesses or guests. In some parts of the British Isles, bread and cheese, biscuits, shortbread or crumbs were distributed, even thrown, to the guests. Originally, a couple fasted before attending their nuptial mass, hence eating after the ceremony broke their fast; food served at a wedding reception today is still called the wedding breakfast, irrespective of the hour.

A bridal cake of flour, salt and water has Roman origins, and was eaten by the contracting parties; originally small individual cakes were sweetened with honey and spices (the inclusion of currants came along later) and shared among the guests. The modern wedding cake is thought to have been devised by a French cook on tour in England who discerned that numerous small cakes could more conveniently be held together under spiced marzipan and icing. In the 17th Century the bride and groom kissed over the cake. The kiss itself originated in the *Pax*, the kiss of peace, following the nuptial blessing after the Pater Noster, which the officiating priest first gave to the bridegroom, who in turn passed it on to the cheek of his bride. In some areas, especially in Scotland, the bride then passed on the kiss to all the male guests. Kissing to signify love, rather than a greeting of peace, was a later development.

Drinking wine (the "knitting-cup") in church at the marriage itself is enjoined in the *Hereford* and *Sarum Missals*; the latter directs that sops be immersed in wine, the liquor and cup blessed by the priest and then the bride, groom and whole congregation join together in drinking. At Whitburn, County Durham a similar custom continued into the late 19th Century where hot-pots of brandy, ales, sugar, eggs and spices were shared in the church after the marriage service. Such "bride-ales" or "bride-cups" were formerly widely enjoyed and in the late 16th Century it would seem excessively so: in a 1547 publication people were advised not to suffer their children "to go to weddings or banquets, for nowadays one can learn nothing there but ribaldry and foul words".

Following the era when the Puritans had succeeded in driving the reception from the church, the wedded couple walked, rode or ran from the service to the jollity. In some parishes a permanent "wedding house", a sort of community centre with a nuptial bed, was built for marital merry-making by all the locals. In some areas it was customary to dash back ("ride the kail") to the festivities, the winner being rewarded with food or drink from the host for giving an early warning of the arrival of guests; this evolved into a "ride for the ribbon", the winner being rewarded by a kiss (or garter) from the bride. On occasions both magistrates and clergy had to curb the fun.

As a sign of the potential fertility and growth of life from seeds it was common to shower the newly weds with wheat (particularly in Nottinghamshire and Sussex); nuts and apples were thrown in some counties. For a few hundred years imported rice was used, and then confetti was substituted to symbolize the seeds. Confetti is the plural of the Italian confetto, a sugared almond originally thrown at carnivals throughout Italy, or distributed in sachets of five nuts to represent health, wealth, happiness, prosperity and fertility. The path from the bride's home to the church was strewn with herbs and flowers, although in some parts of the country fresh sawdust was used to symbolize a new path into married life; this was still practised in Sunderland in the late 19th Century. In Kent items representing the groom's trade were strewn, for example leather clippings for a cordwainer or wool for a shepherd. The bouquets carried by the bride and bridesmaids and the button-holes of flowers worn by the groom, best man and male and female guests, all symbolize fertility and freshness of life, and hence happiness and good luck. The bride tossing her bouquet to the guests is the modern equivalent of throwing her stocking, the latter being a delicate symbolism of having a garter snatched from her at the altar; or the more complete undressing of the bride by the guests prior to her being helped into the nuptial bed - see below.

A chimney-sweep greeting the newly-weds as they leave the church, or at their wedding reception, to bring them good luck in their future, is said to derive from the luck brought to King George III by a sweep who grabbed a team of bolting horses pulling his carriage. George III was certainly Patron of the first Society established in 1796 to end the practice of sending children up soot-choked chimneys, so he brought good luck to climbing boys and girls, even if the story of the bolting horse is untrue.

Exchanging a sandal or shoe was an ancient symbol of change of ownership or agreeing a bargain, as depicted in the Bible in the Book of Ruth [8.15]. Casting a shoe on a plot of land indicated acceptance of purchase, also told in the Bible "Over Edom will I cast my shoe" [8.16]. Hence throwing an old shoe after a newly married couple on their departure, or these days tying one to the back of their car, represents the agreement of the bride being bought by the groom; it is nothing to do with any pagan fertility rite, as some books erroneously claim. It was customary, in some parts of the country, after the bride and groom had departed and an old shoe thrown, for a servant or one of the guests to pour a pan of boiling water on the front door step, thereby "keeping the threshold (or doorstep) warm" as an auspice of another wedding from the same house.

Tolls or fines were informally collected on the wedding day in some parts of the country at a "chaining", "footing", "cock-walking", "pitchering", "petting" or "pennying"; bridegrooms or whole congregations were good-naturedly prevented from entering or leaving the churchyard or passing through the town until they had paid a pet or toll of a penny or more. This custom was practised in Bingley and Wensleydale, Yorkshire into the 20th Century. Pitchering gained its name from the pitcher of water that was likely to be poured over any non-payers. In some places the toll was used to buy drinks to add to the communal merriment, in other places it paid for a football for a match played as part of the celebrations. In Northumberland the couple was locked in the church and not released until they had pushed money under the door; overcoming their first obstacle in married life was, therefore, on hallowed ground. In Burnley, Lancashire, the tolls collected from persons married at St Peter's church paid for the school library books until 1870.

The bridegroom carrying his bride over the threshold of their new dwelling follows an old Roman custom, but is the last remnant of the former marriage-by-capture or rape-marriage described in Chapters 3 and 6. It was the practice in some parts of the British Isles, until relatively recent times, for the guests to witness not only the exchange of vows in church but also the couple entering the nuptial bed. Edward Chicken's poem (see above), towards the end, describes how the families helped the couple to undress. This practice was made more modest by only a stocking or garter being removed which, in turn, became more genteel by the bride removing this herself and tossing it to the guests, as mentioned above. Usually the parish priest blessed the nuptial bed with the couple sitting in it (again with the bride on her groom's left) to enhance the chances of a fruitful outcome of the union.

The belief that a Lord of the Manor has a right to sleep with a tenant's bride on her wedding night may derive from an ancient law imposed by the Scottish King Eugenius III (525-558). He claimed that the monarch should have the first night after marriage of all noblemen's daughters, and that noblemen and heritors of lands should have the same freedom with their tenants' and vassals' daughters [8.17]. The merchet or marca payment to the Lord was to buy off this right. Although this law was abolished in the 11th Century as a result of a campaign by Margaret (1046-93) Queen to Malcolm III, the legend, if not the custom, lingers on today.

Newly-weds going away on their own immediately after the wedding is a further remnant of former marriage-by-capture days when the groom kept his bride in hiding for a period until her family had given up all hope of finding and retrieving her. The rather grander wedding-tour was previously enjoyed only by royalty and nobility; but from the end of the 18th Century, as travel became easier with better road and rail communications, more and more middle-class couples embarked on a honeymoon. The poor, of course, did not, having to return to work directly. Honeymoon is derived from the Teutonic custom of drinking a honey and water cocktail for 30 days (a moon's age) [8.18]. Attila the Hun is said to have celebrated his nuptials gloriously by drinking himself to death on mead (a honey and wine mixture) on his wedding night. 19th Century newspaper reports of weddings often included the honeymoon destination, contrary to today's custom of keeping it from everyone.

Married Life Customs

If a married couple, a year and a day after their wedding, could swear that neither of them had ever repented of their marriage, they could apply, at least on Whichenouvre Manor, Staffordshire [8.19] and in Dunmow, Essex [8.20], for a flitch of bacon as a reward. The Essex custom, established at Dunmow Priory in 1104, was mentioned in Chaucer's *Prologue of the Wife of Bath's Tale* (1390) and continued well into the 20th Century.

The ancient custom of dower (see Chapter 6) evolved into a civil right, expressed in Magna Carta. It was administered by the temporal courts. Even if a wife had been properly endowed with more than a third of the freehold estate, on her widowhood the extra amount was often disputed. The Civil Courts invariably referred part of the dispute to the Church Courts to examine the validity of the marriage or the circumstances of its breakdown. If the marriage was void or annulled, dower did not apply. If the couple separated, say because of adultery, the wife still received her third. If she died before her husband, by English custom and law, her third went to him and his family; in Scotland the wife's terce went to her family. If a widow married again after her husband's death she retained the third from her previous marriage as civil dower was for life. Dower was abolished in 1833 [8.21]. It did not normally apply on a manor as most land-holding arrangements were by copyhold within the feudal system. However, some manorial customs upheld particular arrangements known variously as copyhold dower, widowright, or free-bench. Jointure became a practical solution for a widow by which part of the estate was held jointly by husband and wife; when one died this part was left to the survivor, not to any other heirs. Jointure was then paid annually for the remainder of the survivor's life. In cash terms the annual jointure payment was about a tenth of the original bride-price, the bride's marriage portion (see Chapter 4). In their diaries both Evelyn and Pepys comment on the jointures of various personalities.

The manorial custom of imposing the "leyrwrite" fine for unchastity is mentioned in Chapter 1. Some manors, by their customs and tenures, had a more spectacular method than leyrwrite of dealing with a widow having a bastard child: she

"forfeits her estate, unless she comes into the court of the manor, in the presence of the Steward and all the tenants, and pronounces the following lines, riding on a ram,

Here I am,
Riding upon the back of a black ram,
Like a whore as I am;
And for my Crincum Crancum,
I have lost my Binkum Bankum;
And for my tail's game
Have done this worldly shame;
Therefore pray, Mr Steward, let me have my land again.

Upon this penance she is restored to the possession of her estate for that time" [8.22].

The estate the widow either forfeited or retrieved would normally be held by copyhold tenure, as explained above, according to the particular customs of the manor, while the amount of a widow's estate would depend on any dower arrangements which applied on that manor.

Anniversaries

Even fifty years ago it was rare for a couple to celebrate other than their 25th, 50th and 60th wedding anniversaries. Other anniversaries are more commonly recognized today in the British Isles. Prior to the Second World War, somewhat different tokens (indicated in parentheses) were used. In North America yet further variations have been recognized.

At the anniversary of the year following the marriage

1st	paper (formerly cotton)	20th	china
2nd	cotton (formerly paper)	25th	silver
3rd	leather	30th	pearl
4th	linen (formerly fruit and flowers)	35th	coral
5th	wood	40th	ruby
6th	iron (formerly sugar)	45th	sapphire
7th	copper (formerly woollen)	50th	gold
8th	bronze (formerly salt)	55th	emerald
9th	pottery (formerly copper)	60th	diamond
10th	aluminium (formerly tin)	65th	blue sapphire
11th	steel	70th	platinum
12th	silk (formerly silk and fine linen)	75th	diamond (in North America)
13th	lace		
14th	ivory		
15th	crystal		

Samuel Pepys records in his diary for 1662 [8.23] that he attended two wedding anniversary parties where the guests were offered as many pies as years the couples had been married.

9. Divorce - dissolving a marriage

Divorce as we understand it today, dissolving a valid marriage, was normally unavailable to our forebears. Whether preceded by a betrothal or espousal, marriage was not entered into lightly, and the commitment was infinite. Ecclesiastical and temporal pronouncements over the centuries reinforced this policy. Those who regarded marriage as being a simple promise without celebrant or witnesses realised that mutual agreements between spouses to stay together for the remainder of their lives were binding; they could not be modified by a change in heart or even circumstances. For those who understood marriage to begin at sexual union, once that act had taken place, it could not be undone; hence the couple were married forever. Having made marriage a Sacrament, the Church had no real choice in declaring it indissoluble. Thus both Church and State believed and agreed that wedlock was a permanent bond, to be broken only by the death of one spouse.

But, of course, couples did experience marital difficulties; some wanted not only to be released from their existing unions but to be legally and canonically free to marry again. However, the possibilities were limited. As Archbishop Ecgbert of York clarified in 750 [9.1] "When a woman is dead, her husband may marry another at the end of a month; and after a year [of widowhood] a woman may lawfully receive another husband". This apparent sexual discrimination arose from the practical consideration that men were to remain unmarried for a month out of respect, whilst the year in the case of women was to eliminate confusion over the parentage of any children.

Nonetheless, in many circumstances it was just not realistic to wait for a partner to die. Prior to the Reformation in the British Isles it was theoretically possible to appeal to the Pope or a Papal Curia for a divorce. But such a path was totally impracticable for most people, and their right to use it was questioned by many English authorities. Furthermore, because the end of a marriage automatically made any child illegitimate, thus losing any inheritance, it was also unattractive. The civil authorities were virtually powerless to act, having passed all matrimonial causes to the Church Courts, and so it was left to the ecclesiastical lawyers to find solutions.

There were two legal possibilities: either a judicial separation (both parties went their separate ways, but remained married) or an annulment (the marriage was void from the beginning and so had never been solemnized legally). In the first case an ecclesiastical court could grant a decree *a mensa et thoro* - from bed and board (and mutual cohabitation). Provision was made for subsistence for the woman. As she remained married she was not free to marry again while her husband was still alive - that would have constituted polygamy (see below), strictly forbidden under canon law, but she did retain her dower (see Chapters 6 and 8). In the second case canonical disabilities were unearthed which made the marriage voidable so that a decree *a vinculo matrimonii* (from the chains of marriage) could be issued. Canonical disabilities were situations such as the couple being prohibited kindred (see Appendix II). Any rights from the marriage were forfeited: the woman lost her dower, any children became illegitimate and inheritances could not be claimed.

Simplistically, a voidable marriage had some defect which would normally have been overlooked, but which could be used to declare the marriage null. A void marriage was one in which so many legal requirements had been ignored that it was quite invalid; the couple legally remained single and had no property rights arising from their relationship. Any children were illegitimate bastards and the parents were free to marry anyone they chose (who was legally available).

The judicial separation, or "separation order" as it later became known in a magistrates' court, maintained the marriage but enabled the partners to live apart legally. Conversely, a "Restitution of Conjugal Rights" was needed if one partner had deserted the other but required a judicial decree to return to cohabitation. A later accepted (but dishonest) procedure to obtain a divorce was by "Jactitation"; this required a third party to falsely allege that he (or she) was married to the party petitioning for the divorce.

Generally, therefore, prior to the Reformation and even until 1858, a Church Court made decisions on matrimonial disputes, having examined all the evidence presented by ecclesiastical lawyers. Cases could be taken to an Archdeacon's Court, which might refer them to the higher Consistory Court of the bishop, or a case might go direct to the higher court. The court of appeal from a bishop's court in the Province of Canterbury from the 13th Century was the Court of Arches. In the Province of York the corresponding forum was the Chancery Court. Above the Courts of Arches and Chancery the Papal Court was available until 1533. The High Court of Delegates acted from 1559 to 1832 (with the Court of High Commission), replaced in1833 by the Judicial Committee of the Privy Council until 1858. Many records of these courts survive.

The words polygamy and bigamy have been applied differently over the years. Polygamy originally meant having a second spouse (or more spouses), the first still being alive, which has been forbidden throughout Christendom. Bigamy in the past meant a person having a second spouse, the previous spouse having died; for example, in the 1276 Statute of Bigamy [9.2], "*Bigami*" are defined as men married twice; and that was permitted by the Church and Crown. Gradually, bigamy came to be applied to the original definition of polygamy, more than one spouse at the same time. This was the meaning used in the 1603 Bigamy Act [9.3], and is used by most people in that sense today. Modern anthropologists distinguish between polygyny (one man has more than one wife) and polyandry (one woman has more than one husband). However, both are forms of polygamy which, besides being contrary to Canon Law, was made a felony punishable by death under civil law in England for the first time in 1603 (although it was at that time termed bigamy). It was the polygamous marriages in Ireland (see Chapter 7) with which Church and State authorities were having problems into the 17th Century. The Bigamy Act was re-enacted in 1828 [9.4] but repealed in 1861 [9.5] and replaced by another Act [9.6]; under the latter the punishment (for polygamy) was reduced to seven years transportation or two years imprisonment, although in practice some sentences of death had been commuted to transportation before 1861.

Immediately following the Reformation the Sacramental aspect of marriage was dismissed by some reformers in favour of the original simple contract. They regarded anything which wrecked the basis for the contract as grounds for dissolving the contract itself. Thus desertion, long absence and mortal hatred, as well as adultery, were potential grounds for dissolution: The European Protestant Church, encouraged by Luther, permitted a second marriage in all of the above cases and this view, promoted by Knox, was permanently adopted in Scotland. In England, whilst Henry VIII dismissed the mediaeval canon law of marriage by Statute in 1540 [9.7], in which he reiterated the original Levitical Degrees (see Chapter 2), that Statute was re-pealed in 1548. Cranmer's *Reformatio Legum Ecclesiasticarum*, published in England in 1553, although not admitting spiritual affinity (see Chapter 3) as a ground for divorce, and agreeing that a judicial separation should not be considered as divorce, did support divorce in cases of extreme conjugal faithlessness, desertion or cruelty [9.8]. Even though some English church courts followed its teaching in the late 16th Century, neither Edward VI nor the Church incorporated this into civil or canon law, unlike the Scottish position. But as Dr Emmison has shown [9.9], several marriages took place in England after unfaithful partners had been granted divorces.

However, in 1603 the Bigamy Act did remove just about every cause for divorce from the Statute Book. Adultery was certainly no cause, and now even Spiritual Affinity and Pre-contract were no longer causes, making the conditions more restrictive than in the pre-Reformation times. Nonetheless, the Act made an exception if one party had been "beyond the seas" for seven years and was not known to be alive. Marriage to a third party, in this case, did not constitute a felony: the first marriage was not considered annulled but the Act regarded one partner to have died and so released the other for possible remarriage. The civil courts continued to believe that adulterous spouses or fornicators (the records use the terminology rather loosely) were moral problems of greater concern to God than to the Crown; their punishment was left to the ecclesiastical courts which exercised some severity, though still not contemplating divorce.

From this time it was now technically possible to gain a divorce in England or Wales through a Private Act of Parliament, which on average took about a year. In essence, this replaced the Papal Decree as a means of dissolving a marriage. Such an Act had to be introduced, normally following a judicial separation, through the House of Lords. It could be an expensive process:

£120 if uncontested but up to £800 if contested - yet not the thousands of pounds that some authors have quoted. The damages, of course, could and did run into many thousands of pounds. In the event, from the Reformation until 1700 there were only five such Acts of Parliament (and in 1551 one of those was repealed); and so only four legal divorces in England and Wales in over 150 years. Even until 1858 there were only 330 divorces [9.10] which had ever taken place in the whole of England and Wales.

By 1857 the Church was already losing its powerful influence; for 20 years [9.11] civil marriage had been available, so civil divorce was logical in the eyes of Lord Palmerston and others. Hence by the Matrimonial Causes Act of 1857 [9.12], which applied only to England and Wales, power was wrested from the Ecclesiastical Courts and their lawyers, the Advocates or legal Doctors who frequented Doctors Commons who had hitherto been dealing with matrimonial matters. A civil *Court for Divorce and Matrimonial Causes* was set up, based on the principles of the former church courts, in which civil lawyers were empowered to operate; these lawyers were trained at the Inns of Chancery and Court as described in the Chapmans Records Cameo [9.13] on Education. But it was not achieved without significant opposition from influential laymen (including Gladstone) and the Church (which continued to oppose the principle of divorce for over a hundred years - and some clergy today still refuse to celebrate marriages of divorcees). In 1875 the court became the *Probate, Divorce and Admiralty Division of the High Court*, and in 1967 the Matrimonial Causes Act enabled county courts to try undefended matrimonial causes.

The 1857 Matrimonial Causes Act thus made a divorce from the bonds of matrimony possible in England and Wales based on a decision made by lay judges who were empowered to grant a decree *a mensa et thoro*, and a decree of nullity - though with restricted grounds. Adultery, for example, for the first time (except for the brief period immediately following the Reformation) became a legal cause for divorce. Husband and wife were originally treated differently, but a succession of Matrimonial Causes Acts was introduced to improve the 1857 legislation in 1858, 1859, 1860, 1864, 1866, 1868, 1873, 1878, 1884, 1907, 1919 and 1923 - and then totally revised in 1925, 1937, 1944 and 1950. Under the 1857 legislation the number of divorces rose significantly to an annual average of 277 (1876 - 1880), to 335 (1881 - 1885), and to 500 (1896 - 1900). Between 1946 and 1950 there were 38,000 divorces in England and Wales per year and in 1990 alone there were 153,386.

The Welsh in 943 had quite a different approach to divorce, as can be seen from the laws of King Howel Dha [9.14]. In paragraph 12: " For three causes a woman may depart from her husband, and receive her dowry: if her husband should have the leprosy; if he should have fetid breath; and if he failed to achieve an orgasm". In paragraph 15: "When a divorce takes place, let the goods be thus divided: let the man have the swine, and the woman the sheep. All the vessels of milk, except one pail, shall belong to the woman, and she shall have all the cups but one. The chariot with one yoke, and all the vessels and casks of liquor, shall belong to the man. If the man should soon marry another wife, he ought to send the furnishings from the master bed to the divorced woman. The man shall have the chaldron, the tapestry, the bed, the plough, the axe and the wimble". In Paragraph 18: "A woman may be divorced even for a single kiss given to another man - still more for anything else: and she ought in these cases to lose her rights". From the 17th Century the Welsh recognized a (quite illegal) method of gaining a divorce whereby a wife simply removed her wedding ring in public. She would tell her friends that she was "on lease" (from her husband), and so available for re-marriage (although she certainly was not). "Grace-widow" and "grass-widow" were terms applied in Wales, and elsewhere in the British Isles, originally to divorced women; today, however, a grass-widow or grass-widower has merely an absent, not divorced, partner.

Both the Reformed Established Church of England and the Roman Catholic Church accepted the restrictions placed on divorce after the Reformation, but when the Jews migrated back into the British Isles in the 17th Century they did not; it was fundamental to the rights of a Jew that he could divorce his wife whenever he had just cause - she had few rights anyway.

The Church Court records of matrimonial disputes prior to 1857 leading to separations, or in some instances the cases being dropped, or even to restitution of conjugal rights, were maintained in diocesan or provincial archives. The archdeacons', bishops', and archbishops' courts records all merit investigation. As with probate material the records of the higher courts in general were better kept; and if a case was referred to a higher court some of the evidence quoted in the lower court may have been repeated and noted in the higher court records - useful if the lower court records are now lost. Records of archdeacons' courts and bishops' courts are usually in diocesan archives, mostly in county record offices today. The Archbishop of Canterbury's archives are in the Lambeth Palace Library [9.15], those of the Archbishop of York are in the Borthwick Institute [9.16].

Since 1857, records of divorces - decrees absolute - in England and Wales have been maintained centrally by the Divorce Registry in Somerset House [9.17]. Personal search is not possible but a copy of a decree may be purchased if the full names of both parties are provided. The copy of the decree certificate is actually supplied by the County or High Court where the case was originally heard. Besides the names of the couple the decree gives the date and place of their marriage and the name of any co-respondent. The other records of the hearing, such as details on any children and the final settlement, are not usually provided except to the parties themselves. It is possible, however, that such details were published in local or national newspapers and so are available to researchers from those sources. The Somerset House divorce records from 1858 to 1937 and indexes from 1858 to 1958 are now in the Public Record Office [9.18] but the files (though not the indexes) are normally closed for 75 years.

Another not uncommon, though illegal, method in the British Isles of disposing of an unwanted wife in the 18th, 19th and even into the 20th Centuries, was to sell her at the local market place [9.19]. It was more often, but not exclusively, practised by the labouring classes who believed that publicity was essential for the sale to be recognized and valid. Hence a notice in the local paper before the intended sale and corresponding announcements of successful purchases can be found in local and national newspaper collections. The misconception of legality and publicity may have arisen from the requirement from earliest times for publicity for a marriage - as described in Chapter 3. Whatever the reason, wife sales were often conducted on market days and the sale recorded in the auctioneer's accounts; occasionally parish officers acted as auctioneers. The girl (for the wives were usually less than 25 years old) was normally exhibited with a halter around her neck and the husband selling her passed the reins to the 'husband' buying her.

The arrangements seem to have been quite amicable and when national news was thin were reported also in London newspapers. Very occasionally references to wife sales can be found in parish registers: in November 1821 the register of St Sepulchre's parish, Northampton notes that Mary Adams had been sold by her husband [9.20] to the father (with whom she was then living) of her child, Maria. In the same register, a mere eighty entries earlier William Charles Chapman, 2 x great grandfather of the author of this Cameo was baptised on 8 January 1821 as the son of William and Maria Chapman; frustratingly neither their marriage nor their origins have ever been established. Did they undergo one of the irregular marriages described above - or maybe not bother at all? Research into a number of wife sales indicates that identically to the case of Mary Adams, the purchasers and not the vendors (the husbands), were frequently the fathers of the children of the wives and some pre-arrangements had been made concerning the auctions.

Divorce in Scotland was quite different from the time of the Reformation, as outlined in Chapter 7. The rather complex situation in Ireland is also dealt with in Chapter 7.

Bought a wife on Sunday;
Brought her home on Monday,
Beat her well on Tuesday.
Sick she was on Wednesday;
Dead she was on Thursday,
Buried she was on Friday.
Glad was I on Saturday;
And now I'll buy another.

[*Nursery Anecdotes* - in Jeaffreson, 1872]

Notes and References

More comprehensive names of authors are given in the Bibliography. The formal short titles of the Acts of Parliament are provided against the Acts listed in chronological order in Appendix I.

1.1. 20 Hen III, c.9 (1235).

1.2. 16 & 17 Geo V, c.60 (15 Dec 1926).

1.3. Parochial Registers and Records Measure 1978 - No 2 of the Measures passed by the General Synod of the Church of England which received the Royal Assent during 1978.

1.4. Contact the relevant county record office for details of availability.

1.5. Chapman. *Tracing Your British Ancestors*.

1.6. 7 Wm IV & 1 Vic, c.26 s.18.(3 Jul 1837).

1.7. 15 & 16 Geo V, c.20 s.177 (9 Apr 1925).

1.8. 20 & 21 Vic, c.77 (25 Aug 1857).

1.9. 20 & 21 Vic, c.85 (28 Aug 1857).

1.10. *The Annual Register or a View of the History, Politics and Literature for the Year [—]* began annual publication in 1758 although the first few volumes went into several editions. Marriages did not appear until Vol VI, and after 1862 obituaries were more popular.

1.11. British Library, Newspaper Library, Colindale Avenue, London NW9 5HE.

1.12. 42 & 43 Vic, c.29 (21 Jul 1879), 53 & 54 Vic, c.47 (18 Aug 1890), 55 & 56 Vic, c.23 (27 Jun 1892) and 6 Edw VII, c.40 (29 Nov 1906) are significant.

1.13 General Register Office, Family Records Centre, Myddleton Place, 88 Rosebery Avenue, London EC1R 4QU.

1.14 Public Record Office, Ruskin Avenue, Kew, Surrey, TW9 4DU.

1.15. Guildhall Library, Aldermanbury, London, EC2P 2EJ.

1.16. Lambeth Palace Library, London SE1 7JU.

1.17. British Library, Oriental & India Office, 197 Blackfriars Road, London SE1 8NG.

1.18. Anon. *A Treatise of Feme Coverts*.

2.1. Wilkins, *Concilia Magnae Britanniae et Hiberniae, a Synodo Veralomiensi AD 446 ad Londinensem AD 1717, Accedunt Constitutiones et alia ad Historiam Ecclesiae Anglicanae spectantia* . Wilkins was an archdeacon of Suffolk and a canon of Canterbury. He divided his work into four volumes covering the following periods:
Volume 1: 446 to 1265; in 797 pages, all in Latin.
Volume 2: 1268 to 1349; in 752 pages, all in Latin.
Volume 3: 1350 to 1545; in 877 pages, in Latin to 1521, then some English.
Volume 4: 1546 to 1717; in 806 pages, in a mixture of Latin and English.

2.2 Contrary to the House of Lords decisions in 1844 (Regina v Millis: 10 Cl. & Fin. 534 H.L.) and 1861 (Beamish v Beamish: 9 H.L. Cas. 274). In the former case the decision was historically wrong in stating that the presence of an episcopally ordained clergyman was necessary in the Middle Ages for valid marriage. Even though wrong, this decision had legal binding force and was followed in 1861 in a case which concerned a clergyman conducting his own marriage ceremony. Since 1844 marriage laws in Ireland (ref 7.38 et seq) have been based on that decision. The Lords involved were Abinger, Cottenham and Lyndhurst; those dissenting were Brougham, Campbell and Denham.

2.3. 27 Hen VIII, c.25 (1535).

2.4. Watkinson v Mergatron. Raym. 464.

2.5. References to Wilkins' work (see 2.1 above) are from the appropriate volume with page numbers from his 1737 edition.

2.6. Leviticus. Ch 18, vv 6-18; Ch 20, vv 11-21.

2.7. 25 Hen VIII, c.22 (1533).   2.8. 28 Hen VIII, c.7 (1536).   2.9. 8 Hen VIII, c.16 (1536).

2.10. 32 Hen VIII, c.38 (1540).
2.11. 1 Mar, sess.2, c.1 (1553).
2.12. 1 & 2 P & M, c.8 (1554).
2.13. 1 Eliz I, c.1 (1558).
2.14. Edwards. *History of the Welsh Church.* p 124.
2.15. 10 May 1650 - see Appendix I.
2.16. 10 Jan 1651 - see Appendix I.
2.17. 24 Aug 1653 - see Appendix I.
2.18. 5 & 6 W & M, c.21 (1694).
2.19. 6 & 7 W & M, c.6 (1694).
2.20. Some county record offices hold surviving certificates; see in ref. 2.25 for examples.
2.21. 6 & 7 W & M, c.3 (1694).
2.22. For an entertaining, but not totally accurate, account of the area read: Aston. *The Fleet.* An academic approach by Brown appears in *Marriage & Society;* see Bibliography.
2.23. Chapman. *Ecclesiastical Courts, Officials & Records.*
2.24. 7 & 8 Wm III, c.35 (1696).
2.25. Chapman. *Pre-1841 Censuses & Population Listings in the British Isles.*
2.26. 1 Anne, c.8 (1702); 6 Anne, c.11 (1706); and 6 Anne, c.40 (1707).
2.27. 4 & 5 Anne, c.12 s.10 (1705).
2.28. 10 Anne, c.19 s.176 (1711).
2.29. Weekly Journal. 29 June 1723. (32 couples were married in four days).
2.30. 3 & 4 Vic, c.92 (10 Aug 1840).
2.31. In classes RG7 and PROB 18/50.
2.32. 21 Vic, c.25 (14 Jun 1858).
2.33. 26 Geo II, c.33 (1753).
2.34. 25 Hen VIII, c.22 s.2 (1533).
2.35. Analysed by Colin Chapman and Pauline Litton in 1995; see ref. 3.6.
2.36. 23 Geo III, c.67 (1782).
2.37. 25 Geo III, c.75 (1785).
2.38. 34 Geo III, c.11 (1 Mar 1794).
2.39. 39 & 40 Geo III, c.67 (2 Jul 1800).
2.40. 52 Geo III, c.146 (28 Jul 1812).
2.41. 3 Geo IV, c.75 (22 Jul 1822).
2.42. 4 Geo IV, c.17 (26 Mar 1823).
2.43. 4 Geo IV, c.76 (18 Jul 1823).
2.44. 6 & 7 Wm IV, c 85 (17 Aug 1836).
2.45. 6 & 7 Wm IV, c.86 (17 Aug 1836).
2.46. 7 Wm IV, c.1 (24 Feb 1837).
2.47. 7 Wm IV, c.22 (30 Jun 1837).
2.48. Under 4 & 5 Wm IV, c.76 (14 Aug 1834).
2.49. As allowed for by 4 & 5 Wm IV, c.15 (22 May 1834).
2.50. Office for National Statistics, General Register Office, Postal Applications Section, Smedley Hydro, Trafalgar Rd, Birkdale, Southport, Merseyside, PR8 2HH.
2.51. Marriage (Registrar General's Licence) Act 1970, c.34 (29 May 1970).
2.52. 3 & 4 Vic, c.72 (24 Jul 1840).
2.53. 19 & 20 Vic, c.119 (29 Jul 1856).
2.54. 20 Vic, c.19 (21 Mar 1857).
2.55. 23 Vic, c.24 (25 May 1860).

2.56. 49 Vic, c.3 (29 Mar 1886).
2.57. 49 Vic, c.14 (10 May 1886).
2.58. 61 & 62 Vic, c.58 (12 Aug 1898).
2.59. 7 Edw VII, c.47 (28 Aug 1907).
2.60. 11 & 12 Geo V, c.24 s.2 (28 Jul 1921).
2.61. 16 & 17 Geo V, c.60 (15 Dec 1926).
2.62. 19 & 20 Geo V, c.36. (10 May 1929).
2.63. 21 & 22 Geo V, c.31 (31 Jul 1931).
2.64. 12 & 13 Geo VI, c.76 (24 Nov 1949).
2.65. 7 Eliz II, c.5 (18 Dec 1958).
2.66. 8 & 9 Eliz II, c.29 (13 Apr 1960).
2.67. Family Law Reform Act, 1969, c.46 s.1 and 1st Schedule (25 Jul 1969).
2.68. Marriage (Prohibited Degrees of Relationship) Act, 1986, c.16 (20 May 1986).

3.1. Law Com. 33, para.3.
3.2. Chapman. *Ecclesiastical Courts, Officials & Records.*
3.3. Wilkins . Op cit. Vol 3. p 19.
3.4. Wilkins. Op cit. Vol 3. p 579.
3.5. *A Treatise of Feme Coverts.*
3.6. Extensive research by Chapman and Litton in many hundreds of post-1754 registers of the Provinces of Canterbury and of York shows that within the same rural deanery, archdeaconry or even diocese, no particular printer or publisher was awarded a contract to supply marriage registers; individual printers and publishers were given freedom to interpret Hardwicke's Act and hence required variant details to be written into the pre-printed registers. In some cases the pre-printed banns books and marriage registers were offered as separate volumes, in other cases these were bound together; sometimes the banns in the first half, sometimes the banns in the second half. In some books the banns forms appeared at the top of a page with space for the subsequent marriage entry immediately below. Some books gave complicated guidance as to how the pre-printed books should be completed, others provided examples. Some parishes drew up their own books with hand-numbered pages and ruled lines, which were used for a year or so before reverting to their former habits of higgledy-piggledy recording of information on a couple - and hence by contravening Hardwicke's Act offered marriages of dubious validity, depending on interpretation of the Act.
3.7. Burn. *The History of Parish Registers in England.* p 144; Wrenbury marr. register for 4 Jul 1610 and 22 Jan 1617.
3.8. Chapman. *Using Newspapers and Periodicals.*
3.9. 32 & 33 Vic, c.68 s.2 (9 Aug 1869).
3.10. Law Reform (Miscellaneous Provisions) Act, 1970, c.33 (29 May 1970);
and Family Law Act 1981 (No. 21) s.2 (1).
3.11. Genesis Chapter 2, v 24.
3.12. 4 & 5 Eliz II, c.69 (2 Aug 1956).
3.13. Acts of 1836: see 2.44 and 2.45 above.
3.14. Leviticus. Chapter 18, vv 6 - 18; Chapter 20, vv 11 - 21.
3.15. 8 Edw VII, c.45 (21 Dec 1908).
3.16. Alfred H Huth. *Index Society Annual Report 1878, Appendix 1.* 1879.
3.17. 5 & 6 Wm IV, c.54 (31 Aug 1835).
3.18. Bede. *Ecclesiastical History.* Book 1. Ch 27; also Wilkins. Op cit. Vol 1. p 20.
3.19. Wilkins. Op cit. Vol 1. p 102 (Ex 133 and 139).
3.20. Wilkins. Op cit. Vol 1. p 505. Canon 11.
3.21. 7 Edw VII, c.47 (28 Aug 1907).
3.22. 11 & 12 Geo V, c.24 s.2 (28 Jul 1921).
3.23. 21 & 22 Geo V, c.31 (31 Jul 1931).

3.24. 12 & 13 Geo VI, c.76 (24 Nov 1949).
3.25. 8 & 9 Eliz II, c.29 (3 Apr 1960).
3.26. 1975 Children Act. c.72 (12 Nov 1975).
3.27. 1986 Marriage Act. c.16 s.1 (1). (20 May 1986).
3.28. Wilkins. Op cit. Vol 1. p 102. Ex 131.
3.29. Wilkins. Op cit. Vol 1. p 505. Canon 11.
3.30. Wilkins. Op cit. Vol 1. p 614. Canon 65.
3.31. Wilkins. Op cit. Vol 1. p 219. Canon 35.
3.32. Chapman. *Ecclesiastical Courts, Officials & Records.*
3.33. Wilkins. Op cit. Vol 3. p 430.
3.34. Volterran. Innocent VIII.
3.35. Wilkins. Op cit. Vol 3. p 696.
3.36. Wilkins. Op cit. Vol 3. p 778.
3.37. 2 & 3 Edw VI, c.21 (1549).
3.38. 5 & 6 Edw VI, c.12 (1552).
3.39. 1 Mar, sess.1, c.2 (1553).
3.40. 1 Jas I, c.25 s.50 (1603).
3.41. 12 Geo III, c.11 (1772).
3.42. *A Treatise of Feme Coverts.* p 26.
3.43. 15 Geo II, c.30 (1742).
3.44. 51 Geo III, c.37 (31 May 1811).
3.45. 7 & 8 Eliz II, c.72 (29 Jul 1959).
3.46. Wilkins. Op cit. Vol 1. p 478. Canon 18.
3.47. *Early English Text Society.* Original Series 108. 1897: other instances of marriages of children are quoted by Andrews in *Church Lore*, pp 203-209.
3.48. *Notes & Queries.* 6th Series. vi, 347; vii, 91, 134; viii. 94, 176, 524; ix, 236
3.49. Lazlett. *The World We Have Lost.* pp 81-105.
3.50. The age of 21 requirement was repealed by 3 Geo IV, c.75 (1822); and in July 1823, 4 Geo IV, c.76 restored the pre-1753 rule of Canon 100.
3.51. HL. 90, 66. v.1. Chaired by Lord Ernle (Rowland E Prothero).
3.52. 19 & 20 Geo V, c.36. (10 May 1929).
3.53. Burn. Op cit. p 165 footnote 1.
3.54. Bishop Peter Quivil, Synod of Exeter, 1287: "when matrimony is to be solemnized in the face of the Church. let the priest openly, at the church door, question the contracting parties respecting their mutual consent": [Wilkins. Op cit. Vol 2. p 131. Chapter 7].
3.55. Richard, Bishop of Durham, 1220; [Wilkins. Op cit. Vol 1. p 576].
3.56. 21 Geo III, c.53 (1781).
3.57. 6 Geo IV, c.92 (5 Jul 1825).
3.58. 11 Geo IV & 1 Wm IV, c.18 s.3 (29 May 1830).
3.59. Phillimore. *Ecclesiastical Law.* Vol 2 p 623.
3.60. Wilkins. Op cit. Vol 2 p 175.
3.61. Lyndwood p 274. [Quoted by R Burn in *Eccl. Law* p 467, and by Phillimore in *Eccl. Law* p 629].
3.62. 49 Vic, c.14 s.1 (10 May 1886).
3.63. 12 & 13 Geo VI, c.76, s.4 (24 Nov 1949).
3.64. 18 Eliz I, c.3 (1575).
3.65. 26 & 27 Vic, c.125 (28 Jul 1863).
3.66. 7 Jas I, c.4 (1610).
3.67. 16 & 17 Geo V, c.29 (4 Aug 1926).

3.68. Adoption Act 1952 (no. 25).
3.69. 14 Geo VI, c.26 (28 Jul 1950).

4.1. Matt. Ch.19. vv 3-9; Mark Ch.10. vv 2-12; Eph. Ch.5. vv 22-33; also Brit . Mus. Harl. MS. 4172, f. 62d (written 1426).
4.2. Walter, Bishop of Worcester (1240); see Wilkins. Op cit. Vol 1. p 668.
4.3. Wilkins. Op cit. Vol 2. p 512.
4.4. 44 Geo III, c.77 (14 Jul 1804); 48 Geo III, c.127 (30 Jun 1808); 58 Geo III, c.45, ss.27-29 (30 May 1818).
    59 Geo III, c.134, ss.6,16,17 (13 Jul 1819); 3 Geo IV, c.72, ss.12,17-19 (22 Jul 1822);
    5 Geo IV, c.32 (17 May 1824); 6 Geo IV, c.92 (5 Jul 1825); 7 & 8 Vic, c.56 (29 Jul 1844);
    8 & 9 Vic, c.70, s.10 (31 Jul 1845).
4.5. 4 Geo IV, c.76 s.2 (18 Jul 1823).
4.6. Early v Stevens (1785).
4.7. 6 & 7 Wm IV, c.85 (17 Aug 1836), as modified by 7 Wm IV, c.1 (24 Feb 1837).
4.8. Canon 101
4.9. 25 Hen VIII c.21 (1534).
4.10. Wilkins. Op cit. Vol 4. p 653.
4.11. Wilkins. Op cit. Vol 4. p 659.
4.12. 48 Geo III, c.149 (2 Jul 1808).
4.13. 55 Geo III, c.184 (11 Jul 1815).
4.14. Phillimore. *Ecclesiastical Law,*Vol 2, p 623.
4.15. Lambeth Palace Library, London SE1 7JU.
4.16. Harvester Microform/ Research Publications Ltd, PO Box 45, Reading RG1 8LJ.
4.17. Borthwick Institute of Historical Research, University of York, St Anthony's Hall, Peasholme Green, York, YO1 2PW.
4.18. West Yorkshire Archive Service, Chapeltown Road, Sheepscar, Leeds LS7 3AP.
4.19. Hallward Library, University Park, Nottingham, NG7 2RD.
4.20. Gibson. *Bishops' Transcripts & Marriage Licences.*
4.21. Ecclesiastical Court Dean, 12 New Street, St Peter Port, Guernsey; Ecclesiastical Court Greffier, Jersey;
    Manx Museum Library & Archives, Kingswood Grove, Douglas, Isle of Man.
4.22. Duchesne. *Christian Worship: etc.* p 433.
4.23. *A Treatise of Feme Coverts* p 34, quoting Moor 170.
4.24. Wilkins. Op cit. Vol 3. p 868.
4.25. 2 & 3 Edw VI, c.1 (4 Nov 1548).
4.26. 3 & 4 Edw VI, c.10 (1549).
4.27. 1 Mar. sess 1, c.1 (1553).
4.28. 4 January 1645 - see Appendix I.
4.29. 24 August 1653 - see Appendix I.
4.30. 12 Cha II, c.33 (1660).
4.31. Synod of Westminster (1200), Canon 11; also Clarke p 463, n.4.
4.32. see 2.30 and 2.32.
4.33. see 2.50.
4.34. Institute of Heraldic & Genealogical Studies, Northgate, Canterbury, Kent, CT1 1BA.
4.35. JSW Gibson & Elizabeth Hampson. *Marriage, Census & Other Indexes.*
4.36. Ted Wildy, 167 Carlisle Rd, Browns Bay, Auckland 1310, New Zealand.

5.1. Phillimore. *Ecclesiastical Law,*Vol 2, p 563., quoting 3 Inst. p.89 Fletn. p54.
5.2. 10 & 11 Vic, c.58 (2 Jul 1847).
5.3. 23 Vic, c.18 (15 May 1860).
5.4. 35 Vic, c.10 (13 May 1872).

5.5. 3 & 4 Vic, c.92 (10 Aug 1840).
5.6. 21 & 22 Vic, c.25 (14 Jun 1858).
5.7. Woburn House, Upper Woburn Place, London WC1H 0EZ.
5.8. Mocotta Library, University College, Gower Street, London WC1E 6BT.
5.9. Jewish Historical Society of England, c/o University College (see above).
5.10. Friends' House, Euston Road, London NW1 2BJ.
5.11. Available from Friends' House (see above).
5.12. Chapman. *Tracing Your British Ancestors.*
5.13. Addresses of denominational Historical Societies are given in ref. 5.12.
5.14. 31 Geo III, c.32 (1791).
5.15. 10 Geo IV, c.7 (13 Apr 1829).
5.16. [Catholic Record Society], 114 Mount Street, London W1X 6AX.
5.17. [Catholic Marriages Index], IHGS, Northgate, Canterbury, Kent, CT1 1BA; see also *Family History.* Oct 1991.
5.18. [Catholic FHS], 2 Winscombe Crescent, Ealing, London W5 1AZ.

6.1. Laws of King Ethelbert. cap 76 (AD 605); see also Wilkins. Op cit. Vol 1. p 29. chapter 6.
6.2. Genesis. Chapter 29, v 18.
6.3. Genesis. Chapter 24, v 5.
6.4. 14 Charterhouse Buildings, Goswell Road, London EC1M 7BA.
6.5. Roscow. *Manx Marriage Contracts: 1600-1736.*
6.6. 3 & 4 Wm IV, c.74 (28 Aug 1833).
6.7. 20 & 21 Vic c.57 s.4 (25 Aug 1857).
6.8. Chapman. *Using Newspapers and Periodicals.*
6.9. Chapman. *How Heavy, How Much & How Long?*
6.10. Menefee. *Wives for Sale.*

7.1. Nichols. *Gaelic & Gaelicised Ireland in the Middle Ages.* pp 73-77.
7.2. William Hay. *Lectures on Marriage.* ed J C Barry. Stair Society. 1967.
7.3. Act 1641, c.12.
7.4. 10 Anne, c.7 (1711).
7.5. Act 1695, c.12.
7.6. 4 & 5 Wm IV, c.28 (25 Jul 1834).
7.7. Act 1661, c.34 and Act 1698, c.6.
7.8. Scottish Record Office, HM General Register House, Edinburgh, EH1 3YY.
7.9. GRO for Scotland, New Register House, Edinburgh, EH1 3YT.
7.10. House of Lords unfounded judgements 1844 and 1861; see 2.2 above.
7.11. eg: Smout. *Scottish Marriage, Regular & Irregular 1500-1940*; and Claverhouse. *Irregular Border Marriages.*
7.12. Identical only in principle, as in England the notification for a regular marriage was by publishing banns, or from 1837 giving notice to a civil registrar. In Scotland, notification has now to be first to the civil registrar, after which a regular marriage by a church or civil ceremony can be celebrated; banns have no legal significance today in Scots law.
7.13. Steel. *Sources for Scottish Genealogy & Family History.*
7.14. 2 & 3 Geo VI, c.34 s.5 (13 Jul 1939); postponed by 3 & 4 Geo VI, c.2 s.1 (1) (14 Dec 1939) and put into operation by Marriage (Scotland) Act, Commencement Order 1940.
7.15. 19 & 20 Vic, c.96 (29 Jul 1856).
7.16. Marriage (Scotland) Act, 1939; Marriage (Scotland) Act, 1977, c.15 (26 May 1977).
       Law Reform (Miscellaneous Provisions)(Scotland) Act. 1980, c.55 s.22 (29 Oct 1980).
7.17. 17 & 18 Vic, c.80 (7 Aug 1854).
7.18. 18 Vic, c.29 (15 Jun 1855).

7.19. 23 & 24 Vic, c.85 (6 Aug 1860).
7.20. 41 & 42 Vic, c.43 (8 Aug 1878) amended by 2 & 3 Geo VI, c.33 (13 Jul 1939).
7.21. See ref 7.16.
7.22. Act 1573, c.55.
7.23. 1 & 2 Geo VI, c.50 (29 Jul 1938).
7.24. Divorce (Scotland) Act, 1964, c.91 s.5 (31 Jul 1964).
7.25. Divorce (Scotland) Act, 1976 c.39 (22 Jul 1976).
7.26. Wilkins. Op cit. Vol 1. p 473. Canon 1.
7.27. 33 Hen VIII, c.1 (Ir) (1542).
7.28. Simms. *Frontiers in the Irish Church - Regional and Cultural.*
7.29. MacLysaght. *Irish Life in the 17th Century.* p 48.
7.30. 28 Hen VIII, c.5 (Ir) (1537)
7.31. Decreed in 1152 at the Synod of Kells.
7.32. Ball. *The Reformed Church of Ireland.* p 26.
7.33. PRONI, 66 Balmoral Avenue, Belfast, BT9 6NY.
7.34. The National Archives, Bishop Street, Dublin 8.
7.35. 38 & 39 Vic, c.59 (11 Aug 1875) and 39 & 40 Vic, c.58 (11 Aug 1876).
7.36. Although only four originally-deposited registers survived, many originals were not deposited; copies, transcripts and abstracts of dozens of others are now available.
7.37. Representative Church Body Library, Braemor Park, Rathgar, Dublin 14.
7.38. 19 Geo II, c.13 (1746).
7.39. 33 & 34 Vic, c.110 (10 Aug 1870) and 34 & 35 Vic, c.49 (13 Jul 1871).
7.40. Presbyterian Hist Soc Libry, Church Ho, Fisherwick Pl, Belfast BT1 6DW.
7.41. Society of Friends, 5 Eustace St, Dublin 2;   Friends' Meeting House, Railway Street, Lisburn, Co Antrim.
7.42. 7 & 8 Vic, c.81 (9 Aug 1844).
7.43. 8 & 9 Vic, c.54 (31 Aug 1845).
7.44. 9 & 10 Vic, c.72 (26 Aug 1846).
7.45. 12 & 13 Vic, c.99 (1 Aug 1849).
7.46. 23 Vic, c.18 (15 May 1860).
7.47. 24 & 25 Vic, c.98 s.36 (6 Aug 1861).
7.48. 26 Vic, c.11 s.8 (20 Apr 1863).
7.49. 26 Vic, c.27 (8 Jun 1863).
7.50. 26 & 27 Vic, c.90 (28 Jul 1863).
7.51. 33 & 34 Vic, c.97 s.80 (10 Aug 1870).
7.52. 33 & 34 Vic, c.110 (10 Aug 1870).
7.53. 34 & 35 Vic, c.49 (13 Jul 1871).
7.54. 35 Vic, c.10 (13 May 1872).
7.55. 36 Vic, c.16 (15 May 1873).
7.56. GRO, Joyce House, 8-11 Lombard Street East, Dublin 2.
7.57. Registrar General, Oxford House, 49-55 Chichester St, Belfast BT1 4HL.
7.58. Marriages Act, 1972 (No. 30).
7.59. Age of Majority Act, 1985 (No. 2).
7.60. National Library of Ireland, Kildare Street, Dublin 1.
7.61. Trinity College, College Street, Dublin 2.
7.62. Registry of Deeds, Henrietta Street, Dublin 1.
7.63. Details are in Gibson. *Bishops' Transcripts & Marriage Licences.*

8.1. Law Reform (Miscellaneous Provisions) Act. (1970).

8.2. Stiles. *Bundling.*
8.3. Jeaffreson. *Brides & Bridals,* Vol 2. p 357.
8.4. Piers. *Description of the County of Westmeath.* p 122.
8.5. Andrews. *Old Church Lore.* p 192.
8.6. Wood. *The Wedding Day in all.....,* Vol II. p 68.
8.7. Marchant. *Betrothals & Brides.* p 92.
8.8. Wilkins. Op cit. Vol 1. p 713. [Constitution of Giles de Bridport, Bishop of Sarum].
8.9. Genesis Ch.apter 24 v.65.
8.10. Tegg. *The Knot Tied.* p 299.
8.11. Edward Chicken (1698-1746). *The Collier's Wedding.*
8.12. 18 & 19 Vic, c.60 (23 Jul 1855).
8.13. By the Bishop of Salisbury in 1217 and Richard of Durham at the Council of Durham, 1220;
      see also Wilkins. Op cit. Vol 1. p 581.
8.14. Wood. *The Wedding Day in all....,* p 186.
8.15. Ruth, Ch apter 4, v 7.
8.16. Psalm 60, v 8; Psalm 108, v 9.
8.17. Hamilton. *Marriages Rites, Customs....* pp 167-80.
8.18. Marchant. *Betrothals and Brides.*
8.19. Tegg. *The Knot Tied.* p 224.
8.20. Marchant. *Betrothals & Brides.* p 135.
8.21. 3 & 4 Wm IV, c.27, ss 36 & 41. (24 Jul 1833).
8.22. *Treatise of Feme Coverts.* p 128.
8.23. Pepys. *Diary.* 6 Jan 1662; 3 Feb 1662.

9.1. Wilkins. Op cit. Vol 1. p 108. Ex 118.
9.2. 4 Edw I, c.5 (1276).
9.3. 1 Jas I, c.11 (1603).
9.4. 9 Geo IV, c.31 s.22 (27 Jun 1828).
9.5. 24 & 25 Vic, c.95 (6 Aug 1861).
9.6. 24 & 25 Vic, c.100 s.57 (6 Aug 1861).
9.7. 32 Hen VIII, c. (1540).
9.8. Cranmer. *Reformatio Legum Ecclesiasticarum.* p 26 verso. c 11.
9.9. Emmison. *Elizabethan Life.* Vol 2.
9.10. The Annual Return (123 - s.2:28, 29 May 1857) to Parliament stated 317 but this is quoted in very few textbooks.
      However, even this omitted five that took place that year and other Acts in previous years. Some most mislead-
      ing numbers and commentaries are given in many books on Family Law, and the Royal Commission of 1833
      was incorrect by over 25% in its computation.
9.11. Since the enactment of 6 & 7 Wm IV, c.85 and c.86 (1836).
9.12. 20 & 21 Vic, c.85 (28 Aug 1857).
9.13. Chapman. *The Growth of British Education & Its Records.*
9.14. Laws of King Howel Dha: W 79. b 20.
9.15. Lambeth Palace Library, London SE1 7JU.
9.16. Borthwick Institute of Historical Research,; see ref. 4.16.
9.17. Divorce Registry, Somerset House, The Strand, London WC2R 1LP.
9.18. Ref. J77 (1858-1937), indexed in J78 (1858-1958).
9.19. Menefee. *Wives for Sale.*
9.20. Northamptonshire Record Office. 214P/4; entry 620; 20 Nov 1821.

Bibliography

Works consulted in the preparation of this Cameo:

William Andrews. *Old Church Lore.* Andrews. 1891.
William Andrews (ed). *Curious Church Customs.* Andrews. 1895.
William Andrews (ed). *Antiquities & Curiousities of the Church.* 1896.
John Aston. *The Fleet: Its River, Prison & Marriages.* Fisher Unwin. 1889.
Margaret Baker. *Folklore & Customs of Rural England.* David & Charles. 1974.
J T Ball. *The Reformed Church of Ireland.* Longmans. 1886.
T B Barry (ed). *Colony & Frontier in Medieval Ireland.* Hambledon Press. 1995.
Bede (Venerable). *Ecclesiastical History of England* (written AD 735). ed J A Giles. Bohn. 1859.
Roger Lee Brown. *The Rise & Fall of the Fleet Marriages.* (in R B Outhwaite).
John Southerden Burn. *The Fleet Registers.* J R Smith. 1833.
John Southerden Burn. *The History of Parish Registers in England.* J R Smith. 2nd edn. 1862.
Richard Burn. *Ecclesiastical Law.* Cadell & Davis. 6th edn. 1797 pp 433-512.
Colin R Chapman. *Ecclesiastical Courts, Officials & Records.* Lochin Publishing. 1992.
Colin R Chapman. *Growth of British Education & its Records.* Lochin Publishing. 1992.
Colin R Chapman. *How Heavy, How Much & How Long?* Lochin Publishing. 1995.
Colin R Chapman. *Pre-1841 Censuses & Population Listings in the British Isles.* Lochin Publishing. 1994.
Colin R Chapman. *Tracing Your British Ancestors.* Lochin Publishing. 1993.
Colin R Chapman. *Using Newspapers & Periodicals.* FFHS. 2nd edn. 1996.
W K Lowther Clarke (ed). *Liturgy & Worship.* SPCK. 1932.
Claverhouse (Meloria Smith). *Irregular Border Marriages.* Moray. 1934.
Eric M Clive. *The Law of Husband & Wife in Scotland.* W Green / Sweet & Maxwell. 1992.
Convocation of the Church of England. *Constitutions & Canons Ecclesiastical. 1603, 1865, 1887, 1936, 1946.* SPCK. 1960.
Convocation of the Church of England. *Canon Law Revision 1959.* SPCK. 1960.
Convocation of the Church of England. *Canons of the Church of England.* SPCK. 1969.
J Charles Cox. *Parish Registers of England.* Methuen. 1910.
Elizabeth Craik. *Marriage and Property.* Aberdeen University Press. 1984.
Thomas Cranmer. *Reformatio Legum Ecclesiasticarum.* 1553.
Henry William Cripps. *The Law Relating to Church & Clergy.* Sweet & Maxwell. 1937.
L Duchesne. *Christian Worship: Its Origin & Evolution.* SPCK. 2nd edn. 1904.
Frederick D Emmison. *Elizabethan Life.* Essex County Council. 1973.
Duncan Emrich. *Folklore of Love & Courtship.* American Heritage Press. 1970.
John Erskine. *An Institute of the Law of Scotland.* Bell & Bradfute. 1828.
W Harris Faloon. *Marriage Law of Ireland.* Hodges, Figgis & Co. 1881.
J P S Fergusson. *A Directory of Scottish Newspapers.* National Library of Scotland. 1984.
William J Fielding. *Strange Customs of Courtship & Marriage.* New Home Library. 1942.
Gasquet (Cardinal). *Parish Life in Mediaeval England.* Methuen. 1906.
General Synod of the Church of England. *No Just Cause - Affinity: Suggestions for Change.* CIO. 1984.
J S W Gibson. *Bishops' Transcripts & Marriage Licences, Bonds & Allegations.* FFHS. 3rd edn. 1991.
Jeremy Gibson & Elizabeth Hampson. *Marriage, Census & other Indexes for Family Historians.* 6th edn. FFHS. 1996.
John R Gillis. *For Better, for Worse.* Oxford University Press, New York. 1985.
Mary Goodman. *Wedding Etiquette.* Foulsham. 1966.

Nigel Gravels (ed). *Family Law Statutes*. Sweet & Maxwell. 1992.

R H Graveson & F R Crane (eds). *A Century of Family Law*. Sweet & Maxwell.1957.

W C Hazlitt. *Dictionary of Faiths and Folklore*. Reeves & Turner. 1905.

Augusta Hamilton (Lady). *Marriage Rites, Customs & Ceremonies of the Nations of the Universe*. J Robins & Co. 1824.

Vernon Heaton. *The Best Man's Duties*. Paperfronts. 1967.

H S Q Henriques. *Jewish Marriages & the English Law*. Jewish Historical Society of London. 1909.

Joseph Jackson. *Formation & Annulment of Marriage*. Butterworths. 1969.

E O James. *Marriage Customs Through the Ages*. Collier. 1965.

John Cordy Jeaffreson. *Brides & Bridals*. Hurst & Blackett. 1872.

G H Joyce. *Christian Marriage*. Sheed & Ward. 1948.

Avril Lansdell. *Wedding Fashions 1860-1970*. Shire Publications. 1983.

Elizabeth Laverack. *With This Ring*. Elm Tree Books. 1979.

Peter Lazlett. *The World We Have Lost*. Charles Scribner's Sons. 1984.

Pauline M Litton. *Basic Facts about Using Marriage Records for Family Historians*. FFHS. 1996

William Lyndwood. *Provinciale*. 1432. (trans & ed J V Bullard & H Chalmer Bell. Faith Press. 1929).

Edward MacLysaght. *Irish Life in the 17th Century*. Irish Academic Press. 1939.

W T Marchant. *Betrothals and Brides*. W Hill & Son. 1879.

E Neufeld. *Ancient Hebrew Marriage Laws*. Longmans. 1944.

Kenneth Nichols. *Gaelic and Gaelicised Ireland in the Middle Ages*. 1972.

R B Outhwaite (ed). *Marriage and Society*. Europa Publications Ltd. 1981.

R J (Sir) Phillimore. (ed W G F Phillimore). *Ecclesiastical Law*. 2nd edn. 1896.

Henry Piers (Sir). *Chorographical Description of the County of West-Meath*. 1682. (in *Collect. de Rebus Hibernicus*. 1786).

Frederick Pollock (Sir) & Frederic William Maitland. *History of English Law*. Cambridge University Press. 2nd edn. 1911.

J R Roscow. *Manx Marriage Contracts: 1600-1736*. (in Proc. Isle of Man Nat. Hist. & Antiq. Soc. Vol.X, No.2. 1991-93).

George Riley Scott. *Curious Customs of Sex & Marriage*. Torchstream. 1953.

Alan Joseph Shatter. *Family Law (Ireland)*. Wolfhound Press. 1981.

Katherine Simms. *Frontiers in the Irish Church - Regional and Cultural*. (in T B Barry).

T C Smout. *Scottish Marriage, Regular and Irregular, 1500-1940*. (in R B Outhwaite).

D J Steel. *General Sources for Births, Marriages & Deaths Before 1837*. (Nat. Index of Par. Regs.) Phillimore/SoG. 1976.

D J Steel. *Sources for Nonconformist Genealogy & Family History*. (NIPR) SoG. 1973.

D J Steel. *Sources for Roman Catholic & Jewish Geneal. & Family History*. (NIPR) Phillimore/SoG. 1974.

D J Steel. *Sources for Scottish Genealogy & Family History*. (NIPR) SoG. 1970.

Kenneth Stevenson. *Nuptial Blessing*. SPCK. 1982.

Henry Reed Stiles. *Bundling*. Book Collectors Association. 1934.

Lawrence Stone. *Road to Divorce*. Oxford University Press. 1992.

Olive M Stone. *Family Law*. Macmillan. 1977.

William Tegg. *The Knot Tied - Marriage Ceremonies of All Nations*. William Tegg & Co. 1877.

Edward Westermarck. *History of Human Marriage*. Macmillan & Co. 1891.

David Wilkins. *Concilia Magnae Britanniae et Hiberniae* (see ref : 2.1). 1737.

Sybil Wolfram. *Inlaws & Outlaws*. Croom Helm. 1987.

Edward J Wood. *The Wedding Day in All Ages & Countries*. 2 vols in one. R Bentley. 1869.

Geoffrey Yeo. *The British Overseas*. Guildhall Library. 3rd edn. 1994.

Marilyn Yurdan. *Irish Family History*. Batsford. 1990.

Anon. *Brides*. St Michael. 3rd Imp. 1985.

Anon. *Treatise of Feme Coverts: Or The Lady's Law*. B Lintot. 1732. (Reproduced by Rothman Reprints. 1974).

Appendix I. Some Marriage-Related Statutes

In the following selected list of Statutes, the first reference (in the text of this Cameo) to each Act appears on the left, followed by the Acts in date order, identified in the style in general use until 1963, i.e. regnal year, monarch, chapter number, and occasionally section number, and (date of receiving Royal assent) - thereafter (by 10 & 11 Eliz II, c.34) a less formal style was used, see below - concluding with the [normal short name for the Act, but omitting the word Act and its year of assent].   From and after 8 Apr 1793 (by 33 Geo III, c.13), every Act was endorsed with the date when it received the Royal Assent; this was the date of its commencement unless another date was specified in the Act.   Statutes referring specifically to Wales before 1535, to Scotland before 1707, and to Ireland after 1922, appear at the end of the following selected list.

1.1.	20 Hen III, c.9 (1235). [Statute of Merton]. (Special Bastardy).
9.2.	4 Edw I, c.5 (1276). [Statute of Bigamy].
4.9.	25 Hen VIII c.21 (1533). [Peter Pence & Dispensations; also known as The Eccles. Licences Act of Henry VIII].
2.7.	25 Hen VIII, c.22 s.2 (1533). [Succession to the Crown].
2.3.	27 Hen VIII, c.25 (1535). [Laws in Wales].
2.8.	28 Hen VIII, c.7 (1536). [Succession of the Crown].
2.9.	28 Hen VIII, c.16 (1536). [Ecclesiastical Licences] (Provision for Dispensations etc).
7.30.	28 Hen VIII, c.5 (Ir) (1537).
2.10.	32 Hen VIII, c.38 (1540). [Marriage]. (Precontracting & Degrees of Consanguinity).
7.27.	33 Hen VIII, c.1 (Ir) (1542).
4.25.	2 & 3 Edw VI, c.1 (4 Nov 1548). [First Act of Uniformity].
3.37.	2 & 3 Edw VI, c.21 (1549). [Marriage of Priests].
4.26.	3 & 4 Edw VI, c.10 (1549). [Putting Away of Books & Images].
3.38.	5 & 6 Edw VI, c.12 (1552). [Marriage of Priests].
3.39.	1 Mar, sess 1, c.1 (1553). [First Act of Repeal].
2.11.	1 Mar, sess.2, c.1 (1553). [Declaring the Queen's Highness...]
2.12.	1 & 2 P & M, c.8 (1554). [See of Rome]. (Repealing).
2.13.	1 Eliz I, c.1 (1558). [Supremacy].
3.64.	18 Eliz I, c. 3 (1575). [Putting the Poor on Work].
9.3.	1 Jas I, c.11 (1603). [Bigamy].
3.40.	1 Jas I, c.25 s.50 (1603). [Continuing, Reviving, Repealing].
3.66.	7 Jas I, c.4 (1610). [Against Rogues, Vagabonds & Beggars].
4.28.	4 January 1645. [An Ordinance for taking away the Book of Common Prayer, and for establishing and putting in execution of the Directory for the publique worship of God].
2.15.	10 May 1650. [An Act for suppressing the detestable sins of Incest, Adultery and Fornication].
2.16.	10 Jan 1651. [An Act Enabling the Lords Commissioners....in Cases of Pretended Marriages].
2.17.	24 Aug 1653. [An Act touching Marriages and the Registering thereof; and also...].
4.30.	12 Cha II, c.33 (1660). [Confirmation of Marriages].
2.18.	5 & 6 W & M, c.21 (1694). [Stamp Duty].
2.19.	6 & 7 W & M, c.6 (1694). [Marriage Duty].
2.21.	6 & 7 W & M, c.3 (1694). [Taxation]. (Subsidy).
2.24.	7 & 8 Wm III, c.35 (1696). [Marriage without Banns etc.].
2.26.	1 Anne, c.8 (1702). [Union of Scotland and England].
2.27.	4 & 5 Anne, c.12, s.10 (1705). [Duties on wine etc.]. (includes duty on marriages).
2.26.	6 Anne, c.11 (1706). [Union with Scotland].
2.26.	6 Anne, c.40 (1707). [Union with Scotland (Amendment)].

7.4.	10 Anne, c.7 (1711). [Taxation].
2.28.	10 Anne, c.19 s.176 (1711). [Customs & Excise].
3.43.	15 Geo II, c.30 (1742). [Marriage of Lunatics].
7.38.	19 Geo II, c.13 (1746). [Oaths of Justices of the Peace].
2.33.	26 Geo II, c.33 (1753). [Clandestine Marriages]. (Hardwicke).
3.41.	12 Geo III, c.11 (1772). [Royal Marriages].
3.56.	21 Geo III, c.53 (1781). [Marriages Confirmation].
2.36.	23 Geo III, c.67 (1782). [Stamp Duty]. (Box).
2.37.	25 Geo III, c.75 (1785). [Stamp].
5.14.	31 Geo III, c.32 (1791). [Roman Catholic Relief].
2.38.	34 Geo III, c.11 (1 Mar 1794). [Repealing Duties].
2.39.	39 & 40 Geo III, c.67 (2 Jul 1800). [Union of Great Britain & Ireland].
4.4.	44 Geo III, c.77 (14 Jul 1804). [Marriages Confirmation].
4.4.	48 Geo III, c.127 (30 Jun 1808). [Marriages Confirmation].
4.12.	48 Geo III, c.149 (2 Jul 1808). [Probate & Legacy Duties].
3.44.	51 Geo III, c.37 (31 May 1811). [Lunatics].
2.40.	52 Geo III, c.146 (28 Jul 1812). [Rose's Parochial Registers].
4.13.	55 Geo III, c.184 (11 Jul 1815). [Stamp] (Repealing).
4.4.	58 Geo III, c.45, ss.27-29 (30 May 1818). [Church Building].
4.4.	59 Geo III, c.134, ss.6,16,17 (13 Jul 1819). [Church Building].
4.4.	3 Geo IV, c.72, ss.12,17-19 (22 Jul 1822). [Church Building Act, 1822].
2.41.	3 Geo IV, c.75 (22 Jul 1822). [Marriages Confirmation].
	4 Geo IV, c.5 (7 Mar 1823). [Marriages Confirmation]. (Licences).
2.42.	4 Geo IV, c.17 (26 Mar 1823). [Marriage].
2.43.	4 Geo IV, c.76 s.2 (18 Jul 1823). [Marriage].
	4 Geo IV, c.91 (18 Jul 1823). [Marriages Confirmation].
4.4.	5 Geo IV, c.32 (17 May 1824). [Marriages].
3.57.	6 Geo IV, c.92 (5 Jul 1825). [Marriages Confirmation].
9.4.	9 Geo IV, c.31 s.22 (27 Jun 1828). [Repeal of Felony for Bigamy].
5.15.	10 Geo IV, c.7 (13 Apr 1829) [Roman Catholic Relief].
3.58.	11 Geo IV & 1 Wm IV, c.18 s.3 (29 May 1830). [Marriages Confirmation].
8.13.	3 & 4 Wm IV, c.27, ss.36 & 41 (24 Jul 1833). [Real Property Actions].
6.6.	3 & 4 Wm IV, c.74 (28 Aug 1833). [Fines & Recoveries (abolition)].
2.49.	4 & 5 Wm IV, c.15 (22 May 1834). [HM Exchequer Regulation].
7.6.	4 & 5 Wm IV, c.28 (25 Jul 1834). [Roman Catholic Marriages (Scotland)].
2.48.	4 & 5 Wm IV, c.76 (14 Aug 1834). [Poor Law].
3.17.	5 & 6 Wm IV, c.54 (31 Aug 1835). [Marriage]. (Lyndhurst).
2.44.	6 & 7 Wm IV, c 85 (17 Aug 1836). [Marriage].
2.45.	6 & 7 Wm IV, c.86 (17 Aug 1836). [Births & Deaths Registration].
2.46.	7 Wm IV, c.1 (24 Feb 1837). [Marriage & Registration (delay)]
2.47.	7 Wm IV & 1 Vic, c.22 (30 Jun 1837). [Births & Deaths Registration].
1.6.	7 Wm IV & 1 Vic, c.26 s.18 (3 Jul 1837) [Wills (amendment)].
2.52.	3 & 4 Vic, c.72 (24 Jul 1840). [Marriage].
2.30.	3 & 4 Vic, c.92 (10 Aug 1840). [Non-Parochial Registers].
	5 & 6 Vic, c.113 (12 Aug 1842). [Marriages Confirmation (Ireland)].
	6 & 7 Vic, c.39 (28 Jul 1843). [Marriages Confirmation (Ireland)].
4.4.	7 & 8 Vic, c.56 s.3 (29 Jul 1844) [Church Building (Banns & Marriages)].
7.42.	7 & 8 Vic, c.81 s.83 (9 Aug 1844). [Marriages Confirmation (Ireland)].

7.43.	8 & 9 Vic, c.54 (31 Aug 1845). [Marriages (Ireland)].
4.4.	8 & 9 Vic, c.70, s.10 (Jul 1845). [Church Building Act, 1845].
7.44.	9 & 10 Vic, c.72 (26 Aug 1846). [Marriages (Ireland)].
5.2.	10 & 11 Vic, c.58 (2 Jul 1847). [Quakers & Jews Marriages Validation].
	12 & 13 Vic, c.68 (28 Jul 1849). [Consular Marriage].
7.45.	12 & 13 Vic, c.99 (1 Aug 1849). [Chapels & Marriages (Ireland)].
	14 & 15 Vic, c.97 s.25 (7 Aug 1851). [Church Building]. (Marriages).
7.17.	17 & 18 Vic, c.80 (7 Aug 1854). [Registration (Scotland)].
7.18.	18 Vic, c.29 (15 Jun 1855). [Registration (Scotland)].
8.12.	18 & 19 Vic, c.60 (23 Jul 1855). [Gold Wedding Rings].
	18 & 19 Vic. c.81 s.13 (30 Jul 1855). [Marriages Confirmation]. (Places of Worship).
7.15.	19 & 20 Vic. c.96 (29 Jul 1856). [Marriage (Scotland)].
2.53.	19 & 20 Vic, c.119 (29 Jul 1856). [Marriage & Registration].
2.54.	20 Vic, c.19 (21 Mar 1857). [Relief of Poor etc]. (Banns, Extra-Parochial Places).
6.7.	20 & 21 Vic c.57 s.4 (25 Aug 1857). [Married Women Personal Estate].
1.8.	20 & 21 Vic, c.77 (25 Aug 1857). [Court of Probate].
1.9.	20 & 21 Vic, c.85 (28 Aug 1857). [Matrimonial Causes].
2.32.	21 Vic. c.25 (14 Jun 1858). [Births & Deaths Registration].
5.3.	23 Vic, c.18 (15 May 1860). [Marriage (Society of Friends)].
2.55.	23 Vic, c.24 (25 May 1860). [Marriages (Extra-parochial Places)].
7.19.	23 & 24 Vic, c.85 (6 Aug 1860). [Registration (Scotland)].
	24 Vic, c.16 (17 May 1861). [Marriages Confirmation]. (in Rainow).
9.5.	24 & 25 Vic, c.95 (6 Aug 1861). [Repealing].
2.45.	24 & 25 Vic, c.98 s.36 (6 Aug 1861). [Forgery].
9.6.	24 & 25 Vic, c.100 s.57 (6 Aug 1861). [Offences against the Person].
7.48.	26 Vic, c.11 (20 Apr 1863). [Registration of Births & Deaths (Ireland)].
7.49.	26 Vic, c.27 (8 Jun 1863). [Marriages (Ireland)].
7.50.	26 & 27 Vic, c.90 (28 Jul 1863). [Marriages Registration (Ireland)].
3.65.	26 & 27 Vic, c.125 (28 Jul 1863). [Statute Law Revision].
	31 & 32 Vic, c.61 (16 Jul 1868). [Consular Marriage].
3.9.	32 & 33 Vic, c.68 s.2 (9 Aug 1869). [Law of Evidence].
7.51.	33 & 34 Vic, c.97, s.80 (10 Aug 1870). [Stamp Duties].
7.39.	33 & 34 Vic, c.110 (10 Aug 1870). [Matrimonial Causes (Ireland)].
7.39.	34 & 35 Vic, c.49 (13 Jul 1871). [Matrimonial Causes (Ireland)].
5.4.	35 Vic, c.10 (13 May 1872). [Marriage (Society of Friends)].
7.55.	36 Vic, c.16 (15 May 1873). [Marriages (Ireland)].
7.35.	38 & 39 Vic, c.59 (11 Aug 1875).[Public Records (Ireland)].
7.35.	39 & 40 Vic, c.58 (11 Aug 1876) [Parochial Records].
7.20.	41 & 42 Vic, c.43 (8 Aug 1878). [Marriage Notice (Scotland)].
1.12.	42 & 43 Vic, c.29 (21 Jul 1879). [Marriages Confirmation]. (on HM Ships).
	47 & 48 Vic, c.20 (3 Jul 1884). [Marriages Confirmation]. (in Greek Church).
2.56.	49 Vic, c.3 (29 Mar 1886). [Marriage Validity].
2.57.	49 Vic, c.14 s.1 (10 May 1886). [Marriage]. (Extending Canonical Hours).
1.12.	53 & 54 Vic, c.47 (18 Aug 1890). [Marriage]. (Overseas).
1.12.	55 & 56 Vic, c.23 (27 Jun 1892). [Foreign Marriage].
2.58.	61 & 62 Vic, c.58 (12 Aug 1898). [Marriage]. (Nonconformist Places of Worship).
1.12.	6 Edw VII, c.40 (29 Nov 1906). [Marriage with Foreigners].
2.59.	7 Edw VII, c.47 (28 Aug 1907). [Deceased Wife's Sister's Marriage].

3.15.	8 Edw VII, c.45 (21 Dec 1908). [Punishment of Incest]
2.5.	11 & 12 Geo V, c.24 s.2 (28 Jul 1921). [Deceased Brother's Widow's Marriage].
	13 & 14 Geo V, c.19 (18 Jul 1923). [Matrimonial Causes].
1.7.	15 & 16 Geo V, c.20 s.177 (9 Apr 1925). [Law of Property].
3.67.	16 & 17 Geo V, c.29 (4 Aug 1926). [Adoption of Children].
1.2.	16 & 17 Geo V, c.60 (15 Dec 1926). [Legitimacy].
2.62.	19 & 20 Geo V, c.36. (10 May 1929). [Age of Marriage]
2.63.	21 & 22 Geo V, c.31 (31 Jul 1931). [Marriage (Prohibited Degrees of Relationship)].
7.23.	1 & 2 Geo VI, c.50 (29 Jul 1938). [Divorce (Scotland)].
7.20.	2 & 3 Geo VI, c.33 (13 Jul 1939). [Marriage]. (amending 41 & 42 Vic, c.43).
7.14.	2 & 3 Geo VI, c.34 (13 Jul 1939). [Marriage (Scotland)].
	3 & 4 Geo VI, c.2 (14 Dec 1939). [Postponement of Enactments (Misc Provisions)].
2.64.	12 & 13 Geo VI, c.76 (24 Nov 1949). [Marriage].
3.69.	14 Geo VI, c.26 (28 Jul 1950). [Adoption].
3.12.	4 & 5 Eliz II, c.69 (2 Aug 1956). [Sexual Offences].
2.65.	7 Eliz II, c.5 (18 Dec 1958). [Adoption].
3.45.	7 & 8 Eliz II, c.72 (29 Jul 1959). [Mental Health].
	7 & 8 Eliz II, c.73 (29 Jul 1959). [Legitimacy].
2.66.	8 & 9 Eliz II, c.29 (13 Apr 1960). [Marriage (Enabling)].
	10 & 11 Eliz II, c.34 (19 Jul 1962). [Acts of Parliament Numbering & Citation].
7.24.	Divorce (Scotland) Act, 1964, c.91 (31 Jul 1964).
2.67.	Family Law Reform Act, 1969, c.46 s.1 and 1st Schedule (25 Jul 1969).
3.10.	Law Reform (Miscellaneous Provisions) Act, 1970, c.33 (29 May 1970).
2.51.	Marriage (Registrar General's Licence) Act 1970, c.34 (29 May 1970).
3.26.	1975 Children Act. c.72 (12 Nov 1975).
7.25.	Divorce (Scotland) Act, 1976, c.39 (22 Jul 1976).
7.16.	Marriage (Scotland) Act, 1977, c.15 (26 May 1977).
7.16.	Law Reform (Miscellaneous Provisions)(Scotland) Act. 1980, c.55 s.22 (29 Oct 1980).
2.68.	1986 Marriage Act. c.16 s.1 (1) (20 May 1986). (Prohibited Degrees of Relationship).

| 1.3. | Parochial Registers and Records Measure 1978 - No 2 of the Measures passed by the General Synod of the Church of England which received the Royal Assent during 1978. |

| 9.19 | Laws of King Howel Dha: W 79. b 20. [Wales] |

7.22.	Act 1573, c.55. [Scotland]
7.3.	Act 1641, c.12.
7.7.	Act 1661, c.34.
7.5.	Act 1695, c.12.
7.7.	Act 1698, c.6.

3.68.	Adoption Act, 1952 (No. 25). [Republic of Ireland]
7.57.	Marriages Act, 1972 (No. 30).
3.10.	Family Law Act, 1981 (No. 21) s.1 (1).
7.59.	Age of Majority Act, 1985 (No. 2).

Appendix II. Consanguinity & Affinity Tables

Forbidden partners for intercourse as stated in the Bible:
In Leviticus, Chapter 18, a man's:

mother	mother's sister
father's wife	father's brother's wife
sister	son's wife
father's daughter	brother's wife
mother's daughter	daughter
son's daughter	daughter's son's daughter
daughter's daughter	daughter's daughter's daughter
father's wife's daughter	wife's sister (while wife still alive)
father's sister	

In Leviticus Chapter 20, vv 11-21 a man's:

father's wife	mother's daughter
daughter-in-law	mother's sister
wife's mother	father's sister
sister	uncle's wife
father's daughter	brother's wife

In the New Testament of the Bible the following were confirmed as forbidden:
father's wife (1 Corinthians Chapter 5, v.1), and brother's wife (Matthew Chapter 14, v.4).

The prohibited kindred quoted in 1533 in the first British temporal Statute regarding impediments were:

mother	uncle's wife
stepmother	son's wife
sister	brother's wife
son's daughter	wife's daughter
daughter's daughter	wife's son's daughter
father's daughter	wife's daughter's daughter
father's sister	wife's sister
mother's sister	

The prohibited kindred quoted in 1536 in the second British temporal Statute regarding impediments were:
identical to the above with the addition of "any of the above relatives of a woman with whom he had previously had intercourse". So in today's language if a man had sex with a woman he could not later legally marry her sister etc.

Forbidden kindred stated in the Interregnum Act of 10 May 1650, effective from 24 June 1650.
A person's:

grandfather or grandmother	father's wife
father or mother	mother's husband
brother or sister	son's wife
son or daughter or grandchild	daughter's husband
father's brother or sister	wife's mother or daughter
mother's brother or sister	husband's father or son

Forbidden partners for marriage as stated in the *Book of Common Prayer* of 1662,
(taken from Canon 99 of 1603 and Archbishop Parker's Admonition of 1563).

A man may not marry his:	A woman may not marry with her:
1 grandmother	1 grandfather
2 grandfather's wife	2 grandmother's husband
3 wife's grandmother	3 husband's grandfather
4 father's sister	4 father's brother
5 mother's sister	5 mother's brother
6 father's brother's wife	6 father's sister's husband
7 mother's brother's wife	7 mother's sister's husband
8 wife's father's sister	8 husband's father's brother
9 wife's mother's sister	9 husband's mother's brother
10 mother	10 father
11 step-mother	11 step-father
12 wife's mother	12 husband's father
13 daughter	13 son
14 wife's daughter	14 husband's son
15 son's wife	15 daughter's husband
16 sister	16 brother
17 wife's sister	17 husband's brother
18 brother's wife	18 sister's husband
19 son's daughter	19 son's son
20 daughter's daughter	20 daughter's son
21 son's son's wife	21 son's daughter's husband
22 daughter's son's wife	22 daughter's daughter's husband
23 wife's son's daughter	23 husband's son's son
24 wife's daughter's daughter	24 husband's daughter's son
25 brother's daughter	25 brother's son
26 sister's daughter	26 sister's son
27 brother's son's wife	27 brother's daughter's husband
28 sister's son's wife	28 sister's daughter's husband
29 wife's brother's daughter	29 husband's brother's son
30 wife's sister's daughter	30 husband's sister's son

The 1907 Marriage Act removed number 17 from the prohibited relatives, provided the wife had died - in other words a man could henceforth marry his deceased wife's sister. The 1921 Marriage Act enabled a man to marry his deceased brother's widow, so removing number 18 from the list, provided his brother had died. The Marriage Act of 1931 permitted marriages between a man and his deceased wife's niece or aunt and his deceased nephew's or uncle's widow. Also permitted were marriages between a woman and her deceased husband's nephew or uncle and her deceased niece's or aunt's widower. Thus 29 & 30, 8 & 9, 27 & 28 and 6 & 7 were removed from the list for the man, provided his wife, nephew or uncle had died; and provided her husband, niece or aunt had died in the case of a woman. The 1949 Marriage Act confirmed the 1931 situation and carried the table of 60 prohibited relatives in the First Schedule of the Act. However a different order and more distinctive names were used such as father's mother and mother's mother (for grandmother, number 1), father's father's wife and mother's father's wife (for grandfather's wife, number 2) and wife's father's mother and wife's mother's mother (for wife's grandmother, number 3). Numbers 17 & 18, 29 & 30, 8 & 9, 27 & 28 and 6 & 7 were put into a separate table, indicating that these relatives were prohibited if the affinity link was alive, but permitted if the link was deceased.

Forbidden partners for marriage as stated in the Scottish Act of Parliament, 210, of 9 July 1649.

[C = Consanguinity;   A = Affinity]
A man may not lie with her who is his

3. Gradus inaequalis in Linea transversa ascendente

C. Goodsires (fathers father) sister

A. Goodames brothers (fathers mother brothers) wife

C. Goodsires (mothers father) sister

A. Goodames brothers (mothers mother brothers) wife

C. Gooddame (fathers mother) sister

A. Wifes goodsires (fathers father) sister

C. Gooddame (mothers mother) sister

A. Wifes goodsires (mothers father) sister

A. Goodsires brothers (fathers father brothers) wife

A. Wifes gooddames (fathers mother) sister

A. Goodsires brothers (mothers father brothers) wife

A. Wifes gooddames (mothers mother) sister

2. Gradus in Lineas recta ascendente

C. Gooddame (fathers mother)

A. Goodsires (mothers fathers) wife

C. Gooddame (mothers mother)

A. Wifes gooddame (wifes fathers) mother

A. Goodsires (fathers fathers) wife

A. Wifes gooddame (wifes mothers) mother

2. Gradus inaequalis in Linea transversa ascendente

C. Fathers sister

A. Mother brothers wife

C. Mothers sister

A. wifes father sister

A. Father brothers wife

A. Wifes mother sister

1. Gradus in Linea recta ascendente

C. Mother

A. Step-mother

A. Wifes mother

1. Gradus in Linea recta descendente

C. Daughter

A. Wifes daughter

A. Sons Wife

1. Gradus in Linea tranversa descendente

C. Sister by both Parents or one alone

A. Wifes sister

A. Brothers wife

2. Gradus in Linea recta descendente

C. Sons daughter

A. Daughters sons wife

C. Daughters daughter

A. Wifes sons daughter

A. Sons sons wife

A. Wifes daughter daughter

2. Gradus inaequalis in Linea transversa descendente

C. Brothers daughter

A. Sister sons wife

C. Sisters daughter

A. Wifes brother daughter

A. Brother sons wife

A. Wifes sister daughter

[continued on next page]

3. Gradus inaequalis in Linea transversa descendente

C. Brother daughters daughter

C. Brother sons daughter

C. Sister daughters daughter

C. Sister sons daughter

A. Brother daughters sons wife

A. Brother sons sons wife

A. Sister sons sons wife

A. Sister daughters sons wife

A. Wifes brothers daughters daughter

A. Wifes brothers sons daughter

A. Wifes sisters daughters daughter

A. Wifes sisters sons daughter

No person may marry or lie with those that are in the direct line ascending or descending; or with a brother or sister of one in the direct line; or with the relicts of those in the direct line; or with the relict of a brother or sister of those in the direct line; though never so far asunder in degree: Because all these are Parents and children, or in the place of parents and children one to another. Consanguinity and Affinity impeding Matrimony is contracted by them that are of kindred on the one side, as well as by them that are of kindred by both sides; and by unlawful company of man and woman, as well as by Marriage.

[The original Table also showed those equivalent kindred with whom a woman may not lie].

Appendix III. Sums Payable under the 1694 Marriage Duty Act

The 1694 Stamp Act [5 & 6 W & M, c.21] directly taxed all marriages, as did the 1694 Marriage Duty Act [6 & 7 W & M, c.6] imposed from 1 May 1695 with even wider implications (see Chapter 2). The scale of charges introduced by the latter legislation included 2s 6d for every marriage, payable by the bridegroom [*], on top of which there was a surcharge for those of rank:

£50 for a duke and an archbishop, £40 for a marquis, £30 for an earl and the eldest son of a duke, £25 for a viscount, the eldest son of a marquis and every younger son of a duke, £20 for a baron, a sergeant-at-law, a bishop and every younger son of a marquis, £17 10s for the eldest son of a viscount, £15 for a baronet, a Knight of the Bath, every other sergeant and the eldest son of a baron, £13 6s 8d for every younger son of a viscount, £12 for every younger son of a baron, £10 for a knight bachelor and a dean, £5 for an esquire and a doctor of divinity, law or physick, £2 10s for an archdeacon, a canon and a prebendary of a cathedral or collegiate church, and an additional tax of £1 per marriage for a gentleman and all owners of real estate valued at £50 or more per annum, or of personal estate valued at £600 or more, and all sons of the above ecclesiastics and all younger sons of a baronet, Knight of the Bath, knight bachelor, sergeant-at-law, esquire, gentleman or reputed esquire or gentleman. The sons of those of real or personal estate of the stated values had to pay a surcharge of 10s.

The Act also provided the potential for further income for William III's wars with the French. If the parish collectors (see Chapter 2) did not give a copy of the duty assessment certificate to the incumbent within six days of it being signed by two magistrates, they had to pay £5; and if the incumbent did not read out that assessment in church on the Sunday after receiving it, he was fined £5. Furthermore, if he did not maintain a parish register of marriages (and burials, christenings and births), he was liable to a £100 fine. Parents were bound, under a penalty of £10, to give notice to the collectors within five days after the birth of a child. The outgoing collectors were bound, under a penalty of £20, to deliver to the Receiver-General a duplicate copy of the assessment, with the names of two collectors for the next year, and the names of defaulters on a parchment schedule.

* with 2s. for every birth, and 4s. for every burial, while bachelors over 25 and widowers paid 1s. a year as long as they remained unmarried. Those in receipt of alms were exempt. Spinsters and widows were not mentioned at all in this Act.

Index

* * *

"As a single man, I have spent a good deal of time in noting down the infirmities of Married People, to console myself for those superior pleasures, which they tell me I have lost by remaining as I am.

I cannot say that the quarrels of men and their wives ever made any great impression upon me, or had much tendency to strengthen me in those anti-social resolutions, which I took up long ago upon more substantial considerations. What oftenest offends me at the houses of married persons where I visit, is an error of quite a different description; - it is that they are too loving.

Not too loving either: that does not explain my meaning. Besides, why should that offend me? The very act of separating themselves from the rest of the world, to have the fuller enjoyment of each other's society, implies that they prefer one another to all the world.

But what I complain of is, that they carry this preference so undisguisedly, they perk it up in the faces of us single people so shamelessly, you cannot be in their company a moment without being made to feel, by some indirect hint or open avowal, that you are not the object of this preference".

Charles Lamb. *Essays of Elia.* 1823.